Smothered Southern Foods

Smothered
Southern
Foods

WILBERT JONES

CITADEL PRESS
Kensington Publishing Corp.
www.kensingtonbooks.com

CITADEL PRESS BOOKS are published by

Kensington Publishing Corp.
850 Third Avenue
New York, NY 10022

All Kensington titles, imprints, and distributed lines are available at special quantity discounts for bulk purchases for sales promotions, premiums, fund-raising, educational, or institutional use. Special book excerpts or customized printings can also be created to fit specific needs. For details, write or phone the office of the Kensington special sales manager: Kensington Publishing Corp., 850 Third Avenue, New York, NY 10022, attn: Special Sales Department; phone 1-800-221-2647.

CITADEL PRESS and the Citadel logo are Reg. U.S. Pat. & TM Off.

First printing: May 2006

10   9   8   7   6   5   4   3   2   1

Printed in the United States of America

Library of Congress Control Number: 2005938601

ISBN 0-8065-2745-5

WILBERT JONES

Julia Mae Hogan

To my great-great-grandmother, Julia Mae Hogan (in loving memory); my great-grandmother, Elizabeth Mosley (in loving memory); my grandmother, Ruth Randle (in loving memory); my mother, Thelma Jones; my godmother, Shirley Fields (in loving memory); my surrogate mother, Tessie Garner; and my friend Julia Child (in loving memory). No words can describe you. . . .

Contents

Foreword

WHEN I WAS GROWING UP in the South, I remember seeing so many wonderful foods on our family dinner table. Some of my favorite foods were smothered dishes, especially smothered pork chops—cut thin, browned in a pan, then we would add some flour and water to the reserved juices to make a wonderful sauce served over white rice.

Wilbert Jones, my beloved culinary friend for many years, has brought back that art of *smothering*. His early books proved his love for connecting to those foods that bring us comfort. What I love about his work is that he has a keen sense of taste, yet is concerned with healthy cooking. He was the first to write a healthy soul food cookbook, which showed how traditional recipes can get an extreme makeover, but still have plenty of soul left in them.

Wilbert contributed to *Back to the Table*, sharing his famous smothered catfish recipe. People all over the world have made this recipe time and time again. Let's celebrate Wilbert, who has taught us to appreciate and connect to those foods that bring us comfort and are just darn good!

You will not be disappointed with the many wonderful, great-tasting recipes in this book, and your family will look forward to eating them over and over. My mother, Addie Mae, always said,

"Honey, I'm going to smother you with a lot of love!" Wilbert, thanks for smothering us with your love for food and family.

—Art Smith, best-selling author of *Back to the Table* and *Kitchen Life*, and personal chef to talk show host Oprah Winfrey

Acknowledgments

THANKS TO THE FOLLOWING family members, friends (old and new), and culinary colleagues who are very passionate about food and entertaining.

Christine Randle, Ramona Douglass, Courtney Quiroga, Maryann David, Donna Hodge, Antoinette Fields, Cassandra Banks, Ruth Banks, Nancy Ryan, Charles (Art) Smith, Joyce and Lloyd LeVine, Alva Thomas, Pat Brickhouse, Donna Pierce, Deon Williams, Gloria and Bob Hafer, Charlotte Lyons, Kocoa Scott-Winbush, George and Gale Pearson, Leonard Fields, E. Lynn Harris, Don Browne, Jorgina Pereira, Sonny Lim, Roberta and Rich Trenbeth, Robert and Linda Garland, Frank Garner, Gwen Meeks, Van Woods, Robert and Lisa Nicholson, Charla Draper, Claudie Phillips, LaVena Norris, Doris Odem, Beth Rosenberry, Reid Henderson, Charles Pendleton, Jason and Gwen Swackhamer, DeNita Morris, Burt and Alene Culver, Alan Gordon, Jacquie Bird, Lisa Cureton, Melaine Cooper, Romaine Dauliac, Jesus Salgueiro, Marcus Samuelsson, Royal Allen, Materesa Marshall, Joyce White, Ti Adelaide, Caludia O'Donnell, Gwynne Conlyn, Edna Stewart, Leah Chase, Albert Bullock, James and Kim Butler, Ann McFadden, Vanessa Ruffin, Tina Wilson, Dorothy Barnes, and Ada Penn.

A special thanks to Matt Nielsen at Nielsen-Massey Vanillas and Brian Maynard at KitchenAid.

And very special thanks to the staff at Kensington books, especially my editor, Jeremie Ruby-Strauss, to the copy editor, Navorn Johnson, and to Kristen Hayes, who designed the cover. Thanks.

Smothered
Southern
Foods

Introduction

AFTER DOING EXTENSIVE RESEARCH, I discovered that most Americans are not familiar with the term *smothered*. Those that are live in the south or had some form of family connection in the southern part of the United States.

When it comes to food, hospitality, and cooking techniques, we owe the south a lot of acknowledgment and thanks. Millions of folks around the world have southern roots—including me.

When I think of foods that are linked with the south, I think of shrimp and grits for breakfast; smothered pork chops and rice for a leisurely lunch; and fried chicken, collard greens, cornbread, black-eyed peas, and bread pudding for Sunday's supper. Other foods such as jambalaya, gumbo, she crab soup, barbecue spare ribs, smoked ham, Bananas Foster, pecan pie, and Mississippi mud cakes also come to mind.

My family's roots are in Clarksdale, Mississippi. It is known as the Delta because of its rich fertile soil, thanks to the mighty Mississippi River that runs through the area. Cotton, soybeans, potatoes, and peanuts are the choice crops for this region in Mississippi. Clarksdale is a small town (population of 20,000) that has made its mark on the music world because of the many great blues musicians who were either born there or lived very close by. During my childhood, I spent many weekends with my grand-

RUTH L. RANDLE

2 **Smothered Southern Foods**

parents, Frank and Ruth Randle. On Saturday mornings, I would always get out of bed early just to watch my grandmother cook. I liked watching her through the window or front screen door as she inspected freshly caught fish, delivered by the local fishermen. She would buy fresh buffalo or catfish, always frying it and smothering it with onions, garlic, green peppers, and tomato sauce. I was most happy when she would buy catfish, it was easier to eat, because it contained fewer bones, and the flesh tasted more flavorful (these were fish caught in the open lakes and rivers of the wild).

My grandmother worked as a cook for an Italian-American family for more than forty years. She learned how to prepare many authentic Italian foods such as gnocchi, marinara sauce, and ravioli made with a variety of fillings. Like most great cooks in the south, she mastered the art of cooking by learning to use her five senses. I never saw her read a recipe.

Although Grandmother has been dead for almost thirty years, I still have great memories of her in the kitchen making delicious foods such as homemade parker house rolls. She measured the ingredients by sight, using no measuring utensils. She determined when to stop kneading the dough by touch, never overworking it. She would taste a pinch of the dough for flavor adjustment, then listen to the fire turning on and off in the oven, moving the rolls around so they would cook and brown evenly. Finally, the smell would tell her when the rolls were done just right.

Spending quality time with my grandfather, Frank, was also a real treat. He and I would go to Wade's Barbershop in Clarksdale to get our hair cut. Wade's was the place to hang out on Saturday afternoons, because all of the great amateur and professional blues musicians in the area would pop in for their haircuts. While waiting, many of them would fill the tiny shop with their music. Wade Walton was the owner of the shop, and he was also a blues musician who recorded one hit record in 1958 (that was widely distributed throughout Europe) titled "Shake'em on Down." Wade was friends with the likes of B.B. King, Muddy Waters, John Lee Hooker, and Ike Turner.

My grandfather, Wade Walton, and many of the local and well-known blues musicians have since passed on, but my memories of those Saturday afternoon jam sessions are still intact. Wade's Barbershop has since been turned into a blues museum.

What Is *Smothered*?

The south has greatly influenced America's culinary palate as signature food varieties such as Cajun, Creole, Gullah, Low Country, soul food, and Floribbean have moved from local to national to global. Chef Paul Prudhomme has successfully taken native Cajun cooking to the world's kitchen table. Chef Paul's line of spices and seasonings can be found everywhere, even in the capital of haute cuisine, Paris, and his cooking technique for blackened meats, fish, and poultry is embraced globally.

However, there are still some culinary techniques that have remained regional in this country with which most Americans are not familiar, smothered being one of them. No one knows exactly where this cooking technique came from, but the south claimed it many years ago.

Smothered is a method in which food is covered with another food or sauce while braising in a covered skillet. Smothering is easy as searing a piece of meat on both sides in a hot skillet, then pouring some broth or water over the meat, covering the skillet and letting the meat simmer until it becomes tender.

Many cooks in the south, or cooks who have roots in the south know how to smother food. The south comprises Maryland, Virginia, West Virginia, North Carolina, South Carolina, Tennessee, Kentucky, Georgia, Alabama, Mississippi, Arkansas, and Louisiana.

Florida and Texas are also located in the south, but many food authorities do not consider their cooking style or signature dishes southern. Florida's cooking is mainly Cuban, Haitian, and Spanish influenced. However, the panhandle part of the state, located south of Alabama and Georgia, has a cooking style just as southern as the rest of the southern states. Some signature dishes from this region include biscuits and gravy, fried apples, smothered chicken, smothered pork chops, and blackberry cobbler. Texas also gets dismissed because of its Tex-Mex influences. However, foods such as black-eyed pea caviar (pickled black-eyed peas), pinto beans, barbecue beef brisket, and pecan pie have a traditional southern flavor.

Like the rest of the south, slavery was legal in Texas. Many cooking techniques and ingredients were brought to this state by slaves. Texas was the last state in the union to free slaves, one year after the Civil War, on June 19, 1865. This day led to the celebration of the Juneteeth holiday, which many African Americans and southern whites celebrate today. A Juneteenth celebration often includes some type of prayer service, speakers with inspirational messages, a reading of the Emancipation Proclamation, and food—lots of food!

About the Recipes

This book contains 125 recipes for your enjoyment. They are divided into 6 chapters: Vegetables, Fish and Seafood, Poultry and Meats, Desserts, and Sauces. The directions are simple and flexible. I hope they bring you and your family many enjoyable meals. *Here's to good eating!*

1

Vegetables

About Vegetables

My MOTHER HAD A GREEN THUMB, and she always had a vegetable garden. I have many childhood memories of peeling, shelling, cleaning, and cutting up all kinds of fresh vegetables. Mother grew an assortment of tomatoes, greens, okra, string beans, cucumbers, summer squash, zucchini, sweet bell peppers, radishes, cantaloupes, and watermelons. Many of these wonderful vegetables and fruits ended up in my grandmother's kitchen and were turned into great southern meals.

It's been many years since Mother grew her own garden, and like most Americans, she now shops at the local supermarkets or a farmer's market, as do I. However, from time to time, I like to take a trip to some of the small towns and rural areas in southern Illinois and northwest Indiana to pick and purchase fresh vegetables and fruits from the farmers.

Whether you buy your vegetables from the supermarket or pick them yourself at a vegetable farm, keep the following in mind.

1. Select vegetables that are fresh and firm, not hard or soft.
2. Do not buy vegetables that are old, wilted, moldy, or bruised.
3. Buy peas and beans that have crisp pods.
4. Head vegetables such as cabbages should be solid with only a few waste leaves either torn, browned, or blackened

Selecting and Storing Spring/Summer Vegetables

If you have spring/summer vegetables such as tomatoes, cucumbers, or eggplants on hand and don't plan to cook them immediately, they should be put into the refrigerator or some other cool, dry place. Peas and corn should be cooked soon after they are gathered, because they lose their sweetness. Lettuce should be sprinkled with water and wrapped in heavy cloth or a plastic sealable bag, then put in the refrigerator until ready to use. Cut the stems off wilted vegetables and rinse them in cold water to freshen.

Selecting and Storing Fall/Winter Vegetables

Fall/winter vegetables such as squash, rutabagas, or corn should not be overripe when stored. If they show any signs of spoiling, remove them from the other vegetables. Pick vegetables that are in good condition, then store them in a cool, dry, well-ventilated place. Most vegetables last longer if they are stored spread out so that they do not touch each other. Squash and sweet potatoes require a warmer storage temperature than other vegetables. Parsnips improve in flavor if they are stored frozen.

Buttery Beets

This recipe calls for fresh beets. If they are not available, use canned beets, drained of their juices. Only ten minutes of cooking time is required for canned beets.

1 pound fresh beets
½ cup butter
½ teaspoon salt

¼ teaspoon garlic powder
¼ teaspoon onion powder

Cut the tops off the beets, wash them, and peel their skins off with a sharp knife or potato peeler. Shred the beets in a food processor and set aside. Melt the butter in a medium-size saucepan over medium heat. Pour the shredded beets in the pan, season with salt, garlic powder, and onion powder. Cover the saucepan with a lid and let simmer for 20 minutes or until tender.

Makes 4 to 6 servings.

Corn and Peanuts

This recipe can be spiced up by adding one or two green or red chili peppers and about ¼ teaspoon ground red (cayenne) pepper. Toasted pine nuts or roasted pecans can be substituted for the roasted peanuts.

4 cups fresh or frozen corn
    kernels
1 cup diced onions
2 tablespoons butter or
    vegetable oil
1 cup unsalted roasted
    peanuts

½ teaspoon salt
½ teaspoon black pepper
¼ cup freshly chopped
    parsley

Place all the ingredients except the parsley in a large skillet. Add ½ cup water, and heat over medium heat until the corn mixture is hot. Reduce the heat to low, cover the skillet with a lid, and let simmer about 15 minutes or until the corn kernels are tender.

Makes 4 servings.

Cucumbers and Zucchini

This recipe calls for cucumbers and zucchini to be served hot, but it can also be served as a chilled soup. Just puree it after it has cooked and cooled down. If serving as a chilled soup, garnish it with sour cream and wedges of fresh lemons.

2 tablespoons olive oil
1 tablespoon butter
2 medium-size cucumbers, peeled, seeded, and cut into ½-inch slices
2 medium-size zucchini, peeled, seeded, and cut into ½-inch slices

2 tablespoons fresh tarragon
1 tablespoon fresh thyme
1 cup heavy cream
½ teaspoon salt
¼ teaspoon black pepper

Heat the olive oil and butter in a large frying pan over medium heat until the butter is melted. Add the cucumber and zucchini slices and sauté them about 3 or 4 minutes or until they are tender. Add the tarragon, thyme, heavy cream, salt, and pepper; cover the frying pan with a lid and let simmer about 15 minutes, stirring occasionally. Garnish with ¼ cup sliced green onions (scallions).

Makes 4 to 6 servings.

Green Beans with Tomatoes

There's nothing better than having vegetables picked out of a garden in the early part of spring. I always make this dish as if it were an annual rite of passage to the spring. Different variations can be made by adding fresh mushrooms, zucchini, or okra.

1 pound fresh string beans	½ teaspoon sugar
2 cups dry white wine	1 teaspoon salt
2 cups freshly chopped tomatoes	½ teaspoon black pepper

Wash and clip the ends of the string beans and set aside. Pour the wine, chopped tomatoes, sugar, salt, and black pepper in a large saucepan or Dutch oven. Bring to a boil, then add the string beans along with ½ cup of water. Cover the saucepan with a lid and let simmer about 20 minutes or until the beans are tender. Serve hot, or chill in the refrigerator and serve as a cold bean salad.

Makes 4 to 6 servings.

Green Tomatoes and
Mushrooms

If green tomatoes are not available, red tomatoes can be used in this recipe, but use firm ones. Once this dish is made, it can be served over baked potatoes or grits, and can be stored in the freezer for up to two months.

5 strips bacon, cut into 1-inch
  pieces
1 cup diced onions
1 cup chopped celery
2 pounds (4 large or 6
  medium) chopped green
  tomatoes

1 pound coarsely chopped
  white button mushrooms
2 cups fresh or frozen corn
  kernels
½ teaspoon dried thyme
3 dashes Tabasco sauce
  (optional)

Place the bacon in a large, heavy-bottomed skillet or Dutch oven and sauté over medium heat until crispy and brown. Drain the cooked pieces on paper towels. Stir the remaining ingredients into the bacon drippings in the pan, cover the skillet with a lid, and reduce the heat to low. Simmer 25 to 30 minutes or until the vegetables are tender. Stir in the bacon.

Makes 6 to 8 servings.

Hot Slaw

I was a teenager when I first tried Hot Slaw. I had it on a chicken sandwich, and the taste was even better than the name suggests. Try it on a grilled hamburger or a chicken sandwich, or on top of baked beans or baked pork chops.

4 cups shredded cabbage
2 cups shredded carrots
1½ cups vegetable broth or
  chicken broth
2 tablespoons vinegar

1 teaspoon sugar
¼ teaspoon sweet paprika
½ teaspoon salt
1½ cups heavy cream

Place the shredded cabbage and shredded carrots in a large sauté pan. Add the broth and vinegar, and cook over medium heat about 5 minutes, constantly stirring. Cover the sauté pan with a lid and let simmer about 15 minutes or until the cabbage and carrots are tender. Remove the lid, stir in the remaining ingredients, and cook until the sauce turns thick.

Makes 6 to 8 servings.

Lima Beans with Water Chestnuts

Black-eyed peas or Northern beans can be substituted for the lima beans in this recipe. Fresh beans are recommended; however, if they are not available, use frozen ones.

1 pound fresh lima beans
2 cups canned, sliced water
   chestnuts
1 tablespoon freshly chopped
   thyme

4 cups vegetable broth
½ cup bottled Italian salad
   dressing

Place all the ingredients except the Italian salad dressing in a large, heavy-bottomed skillet or Dutch oven. Cook over medium heat 15 minutes, then cover the skillet with a lid and let simmer about 30 minutes or until the beans are tender. Pour the beans in a serving bowl, leaving the reserve liquid in the skillet. Pour the Italian salad dressing over the beans and stir well.

Makes 6 to 8 servings.

Potatoes and Bacon

The first time I had this recipe it was made with sweet potatoes instead of white potatoes. I was about nine years old at the time, and I thought it was a dessert because of the sweetness of the potatoes. Years later, when I started cooking, I came up with this version of potatoes and bacon. When making this recipe, I recommend using a good-quality bacon, or substituting smoked chicken breast or smoked turkey breast—preferably from a butcher.

1 pound bacon, cut into 1-inch pieces
1 cup chopped sweet red bell peppers
1 cup chopped sweet yellow bell peppers
4 cups white potatoes, peeled, cut into ½-inch cubes
2 cups chicken or vegetable broth
salt and black pepper to taste
½ cup freshly chopped parsley

Place the bacon pieces in a large, heavy-bottomed skillet or Dutch oven and cook over medium heat until they are brown and crispy. Drain on paper towels and set aside. Place the red and yellow peppers and potatoes in the reserved bacon drippings and sauté for about 5 minutes. Pour in the chicken broth, cover the skillet with a lid, and let simmer for about 15 minutes or until the vegetables turn soft. Stir in the cooked bacon pieces; season with salt and pepper to taste. Garnish with parsley and serve.

Makes 4 to 6 servings.

Spinach and Garlic

Swiss chard, kale, or beet greens (the green leaves and stems attached to fresh beets) can be substituted for the spinach in this recipe. Be sure to choose young, tender leaves—avoid limp, dry, or yellowed leaves and woody stalks, which show that the greens are old.

2 tablespoons olive oil	2 pounds fresh spinach,
2 tablespoons butter	washed and drained
2 tablespoons finely chopped	½ teaspoon black pepper
garlic	¼ teaspoon ground nutmeg

Heat the olive oil and butter in a large saucepan over medium heat about 2 minutes until hot. Add the chopped garlic and sauté until it turns light brown (not dark). Stir in the remaining ingredients, cover the saucepan with a lid, and let simmer 20 minutes, stirring occasionally.

Makes 4 to 6 servings.

Yellow Squash and Carrots

Yellow squash, sometimes called summer squash, are usually available in the stores and farmer's markets from late spring to early fall. When selecting them, be sure the skin is unbroken and has no soft or brown patches. Also note that the squash's flavor decreases as its size increases.

2 tablespoons olive oil

2 pounds yellow squash, peeled and cut into ¼-inch slices

1 pound carrots, peeled and sliced into ¼-inch slices

1 cup vegetable broth

¼ cup chopped fresh dill

½ teaspoon salt

½ teaspoon black pepper

Heat the olive oil in a large frying pan over medium heat for 1 minute until it turns hot. Add the squash and carrots and sauté about 10 minutes. Add the remaining ingredients, cover, and let simmer about 20 to 25 minutes or until the vegetables are tender, stirring occasionally.

Makes 6 to 8 servings.

<hr/>

Asparagus, Mushrooms, and Onions

This recipe takes me back about twenty years, when I was having dinner with my good friend Romaine Dauliac and his family. We dined at the famed La Closerie des Lilas Restaurant in Paris. This restaurant is a landmark institution in Paris, with more than eighty years under its belt. During the early part of the twentieth century, La Closerie des Lilas was a regular spot for Josephine Baker, Richard Wright, and Ernest Hemingway. My dinner entrée was a tasty dish called La Cote de Veau Poelee aux Champignons et Asperges (Veal Chop with Wild Mushrooms and Asparagus). It was wonderful! About ten years ago, I came up with this modified version with a slight southern flair. It's a vegetarian version, but just as tasty.

14 green asparagus stalks,
     tough ends cut off,
     blanched 3 minutes in
     boiling water
⅓ cup butter
2 tablespoons olive oil
1 cup diced sweet potatoes,
     washed and peeled
1 cup chopped oyster
     mushrooms, brushed
     clean

1 cup chopped chanterelle
     mushrooms, brushed
     clean
10 small onions (pearl onions
     can be used)
2 tablespoons chopped garlic
salt and black pepper to taste

Cut the asparagus into 1½-inch pieces and set aside. Heat the butter and oil in a large skillet over medium heat for 2 minutes until hot. Add the asparagus, sweet potatoes, mushrooms, onions, and garlic. Cover, reduce the heat to low, and cook for 15 minutes. Remove the lid and sprinkle in the salt and pepper, replace the lid and cook 3 minutes longer or until the vegetables are soft.

Makes 4 to 6 servings.

Barbecued Potatoes

This recipe works best when using large red potatoes, which are available year round.

2 pounds (4 to 6) large red
     potatoes
3 cups peanut oil, for frying

1½ cups Barbecue Sauce, see
     recipe on page 127
salt to taste

Wash the potatoes, peel, and cut into ¼-inch sticks, about 3 inches long. Place them in cold water to prevent discoloration and to soak out some of the starch. A little salt can be added to the water to keep the potatoes firm until use.

Heat the peanut oil to 375°F in a large pot or Dutch oven. Place the potato sticks in a large colander to drain the water, then pat them dry with paper towels and place in the hot oil. Fry for about 2 minutes or until they are golden brown and crispy. Drain on paper towels and sprinkle lightly with salt.

Heat the barbecue sauce in a large saucepan over medium heat until it starts to boil. Add the fried potatoes, cover, and let simmer for about 3 minutes. Serve with toasted garlic bread or plain white bread.

Makes 6 servings.

Beets and Onions

I recommend using fresh beets for this recipe. The green tops are usually cut off before the beets reach grocery stores. When they are attached, most people usually toss them out because they don't know how to cook them or use them in a recipe. However, they are very easy to cook.

I once had a delicious brunch at a bed & breakfast in Natchez, Mississippi, and one of the dishes served was chopped beet stems and leaves sautéed in olive oil, fresh thyme, chopped wild mushrooms, salt, and pepper. Beet tops are very good to eat, and they are loaded with nutrients, vitamins, and minerals. If available, fresh beet greens can be chopped up and cooked with the beets and onions in this recipe.

¼ cup vegetable oil
1 pound fresh beets, peeled
    and cut into ½-inch cubes
    (if canned, drained)
1½ cups diced onions

10 garlic cloves
¼ teaspoon ground cumin
salt and black pepper to taste
1 cup dry red wine
½ teaspoon cornstarch

Heat the oil in a large non-stick sauté pan over medium heat for 2 minutes or until hot. Add the beets, onions, and garlic cloves, and sauté about 5 minutes or until the vegetables turn soft. Sprinkle in the cumin, salt, and pepper and pour in the wine. Reduce the heat to low, cover, and let simmer about 10 minutes. Stir in the corn starch to make a slightly thick sauce.

Makes 4 servings.

Buttered Brown Potatoes

Instead of the baby (new) potatoes, sweet potatoes can be used in this recipe. When I wrote my first cookbook, *The New Soul Food Cookbook*, ten years ago, I developed a recipe for baked sweet potato chips that called for rosemary sprinkled on the sweet potato slices before they were baked—it turned out to be a big hit. The sweetness of the sweet potatoes complemented the earthy taste of the rosemary.

2 pounds new potatoes (baby potatoes) or sweet potatoes, cut into 2-inch pieces
⅓ cup vegetable oil
½ teaspoon dried rosemary
1 teaspoon dried marjoram

½ teaspoon white pepper
¼ teaspoon crushed red pepper flakes
½ cup butter, melted
1 cup half & half
1 cup vegetable broth

Peel the potatoes and cut them into 2-inch pieces. Combine all the ingredients except the butter, half & half, and vegetable broth in a large mixing bowl; mix well to make sure that the potatoes are coated. Heat a large skillet over medium heat about 2 minutes. Add the coated potatoes to the heated skillet and cook about 5 minutes or until the potatoes become tender and slightly brown, stirring constantly so that they don't stick to the bottom of the skillet. Add the melted butter, half & half, and vegetable broth, cover, and cook about 10 to 12 minutes.

Makes 4 to 6 servings.

Buttered Kale

Kale was not one of the greens that I grew up eating. Most Mississippians who lived in the Delta ate collard, cabbage, mustard, turnip, and dandelion greens, and sometimes the wild pokeweed.

I was an adult when I had my first pot of kale greens. Now I'm in love with them, especially curly kale, which looks like a curly dark mustard green, but has a much stronger, earthy flavor.

4 bunches kale	1 cup carrots, peeled and
½ cup butter	chopped into ⅛-inch
¼ cup cider vinegar	slices
salt, to taste	6 slices smoked bacon, cut
2 large onions, peeled and cut	into ½-inch pieces
into ¼-inch slices	

Place all the ingredients in a large saucepan and add about 3 cups of water. Bring to a boil; reduce heat to medium, cover, and let simmer about 1 hour or until the greens are tender. Serve with some freshly made cornbread.

Makes 6 servings.

Buttered Turnips

Southerners usually don't like cooking what we call "naked greens" (greens cooked with no meat). But occasionally, my grandmother cooked a pot of fresh, young naked turnip greens, with turnips. Turnips have a delicate, slightly sweet flavor that becomes stronger as they age, but still taste great. I also like them sauteéd in olive oil or cooked in broth and butter.

2½ pounds turnips
¼ cup butter
2 tablespoons freshly
   chopped garlic
1 cup chopped sweet red bell
   peppers

1 cup chopped sweet yellow
   bell peppers
1½ cups vegetable broth
salt and black pepper to taste

Peel the turnips, cut them into ½-inch slices, and place them in a large bowl covered with water to prevent discoloration. Melt the butter over medium heat in a large sauté pan or skillet. Add the turnip slices, garlic, and red and yellow bell peppers, and sauté for about 10 minutes or until the vegetables are semi-soft. Add the vegetable broth, salt, and pepper, cover and reduce the heat to low, and let simmer for 10 to 12 minutes or until the vegetables become soft.

Makes 6 servings.

Cabbage and Smoked Turkey

The flavor of smoked turkey has come a long way. Most of us remember, about twenty-five years ago, when the taste of it was terrible. At that time, there were only a few manufacturers that produced turkey products, and it seemed that they were not too concerned with the quality—it was cured with a lot of salt, and once boiled, all of its flavor disappeared. At that time, pork was the chosen meat for seasoning most foods, especially in southern cooking.

Gradually, consumers started demanding healthier foods from the grocery stores, which eventually led to producers manufacturing better-quality, better-tasting products, especially smoked turkey. Nowadays, you can fool many die-hard pork lovers by substituting smoked turkey in their favorite dishes such as greens, black-eyed peas, or pinto beans.

1½ pounds smoked turkey (legs or wings)	2 tablespoons cider vinegar
2 heads cabbage (about 1 pound each)	1 teaspoon black pepper
	1 jalapeño pepper, cut lengthwise (optional)

Wash the turkey meat under cold water and pat dry. Using a sharp knife, cut a few long slits through the skin (this technique shortens the cooking time). Place the smoked turkey meat in a large saucepan or Dutch oven and cover with water. Bring to a boil over high heat, then reduce the heat to medium, cover, and let simmer about 1 hour or until the meat is tender. Add the cabbage, vinegar, black pepper, and jalapeño pepper; cover again, and let simmer 45 to 50 minutes or until the cabbage is tender, but not mushy.

Makes 6 to 8 servings.

Cajun Buttered Beans

On March 14, 1996, my cousin Christine Randle and I went on one of our food trips. We went to New Orleans to feast at Paul Prudhomme's restaurant, K-Paul's Louisiana Kitchen. In my opinion, it was Chef Paul who put Cajun cooking on the international map. This would be my first visit to his restaurant, so I was looking forward to the experience. But hours before we were scheduled to arrive, Chef Paul became sick and had to go home. His sous chef cooked for us that evening—and it was wonderful. My cousin and I tried almost everything on the menu, especially all of Paul's signature dishes such as Cajun Salmon and Jambalaya. Paul has since broadened his culinary trade. He has a line of successful spices and seasonings that captures all the flavors of Louisiana, not just Cajun.

This recipe of Cajun Buttered Beans reminds me of that very day, in Paul Prudhomme's restaurant.

4 cups fresh butter beans
2 cups fresh corn kernels
1 cup finely chopped
    portabella mushrooms
½ cup melted butter
2 cups chicken or vegetable
    broth

2 tablespoons commercial
    Cajun seasoning
¼ teaspoon dried thyme
1 teaspoon file powder (see
    below)

Place all the ingredients except the file powder, in a large, heavy-bottomed skillet or a Dutch oven. Add about 2 cups of water and bring to a boil over high heat, then reduce heat to medium and cover. Cook about 40 to 45 minutes or until the beans are soft. Stir in the file powder and serve.

Makes 4 to 6 servings.

Note: File powder can be purchased in specialty or ethnic stores. Its made from the leaves of the sassafras tree, and it is used in a lot of Creole and Cajun dishes as a thickener and flavor enhancer. Never add file powder to a dish before or during cooking—it gives the dish a bitter aftertaste.

Chili Kidney Beans

I enjoy this dish with a piece of buttermilk cornbread. I've also served it over hot dog and hamburger buns, and, occasionally, I add about 2 cups of ground pork, ground chicken, or ground Italian sausage to it. It's a very versatile recipe, so be creative.

2 14-oz cans kidney beans, drained
1 cup diced onions
1½ cups fresh corn kernels
1 cup diced sweet green bell peppers
3 cups Tomato Sauce, see recipe on page 133
1 cup diced tomatoes
1 tablespoon dark chili powder
½ teaspoon ground coriander
2 tablespoons dark molasses
1 cup shredded sharp cheddar cheese
¼ cup sour cream
2 tablespoons finely chopped jalapeño peppers (optional)

Place the beans, onions, corn, green bell peppers, tomato sauce, diced tomatoes, chili powder, ground coriander and molasses in a large pot or Dutch oven. Cover, and let simmer over medium heat about 30 minutes, stirring occasionally. Place the chili in a large serving bowl, and top with cheddar cheese, sour cream, and chopped jalapeño peppers.

Makes 6 servings.

Corn and Tomatoes

Born in the 1880s in Mississippi, my great-grandmother, Ada Penn (we called her Grandma Ada), used to make some of the most beautiful quilts from old scraps of fabric, including our old clothes that we outgrew. She would create many types of pattern designs. Sadly, I never got a chance to ask her about whether the pattern designs that she used had any symbolic meanings.

Years later, I ran across a book called *Hidden in Plain View: A Secret Story of Quilts and the Underground Railroad* by Jacqueline Tobin and Raymond Dobard. The book described quilts containing hidden messages and secret symbols used to assist slaves with locating the Underground Railroad trail.

My mother has one of Grandma Ada's quilts left, but due to its decades of use, no patterns or symbols can be recognized. So, we'll never know if Grandma Ada used hidden messages and secret symbols in her quilts. What a pity.

This recipe for Corn and Tomatoes reminds me of a quilt, made with lots of love. Like a quilt pattern, many ingredients can be added to it (fish, chicken, pork, or other vegetables) to create different flavors.

3 cups fresh corn kernels	½ cup melted butter
2 cups diced tomatoes	1 tablespoon sugar
¼ cup diced sweet green bell peppers	¼ teaspoon dried thyme
	½ teaspoon salt
¼ cup diced onions	½ teaspoon black pepper

Place the corn, tomatoes, green bell peppers, and onion in a large, heavy-bottomed skillet. Cover the skillet and cook about 5 minutes over high heat, stirring frequently. Add the butter, sugar, thyme, salt, and black pepper. Cover again, reduce the heat to low, and cook about 15 minutes or until the corn and bell peppers are tender.

Makes 6 servings.

Creamed Mushrooms

When I was about sixteen years old, I remember making spaghetti with a mushroom sauce that was very watery with a weak flavor. I'd washed the mushrooms in a lot of water, so when I started to chop them up, the water they had absorbed made my spaghetti sauce too thin and weak tasting. Mushrooms are like sponges and will soak up whatever liquid you put them in. I tossed out the sauce and made it over again, this time cleaning the mushrooms with damp towels. That was an expensive lesson to learn—twenty-five years ago, mushrooms were not as cheap as they are today. Remember, clean your mushrooms with damp paper towels or a damp pastry brush—don't wash them.

½ pound portabella
   mushrooms
½ pound white button
   mushrooms
½ pound oyster mushrooms
2 tablespoons olive oil
¼ cup chopped shallots
2 cups heavy cream

salt and black pepper to taste
½ teaspoon crushed red
   pepper flakes
½ cup freshly grated
   Parmesan cheese
¼ cup Italian seasoned bread
   crumbs

Using moist paper towels, wipe the dirt from the mushrooms, then chop coarsely and set aside. Heat the olive oil in a large sauté pan over medium heat for about 2 minutes or until hot (not smoky). Add the shallots and sauté for about 1 minute. Add the cleaned, chopped mushrooms and sauté for about 3 minutes. Pour in the cream, red pepper flakes, salt, and black pepper. Cover the pan, reduce heat to low, and let simmer for 10 minutes. Turn the heat off and stir in the grated Parmesan cheese. Sprinkle the bread crumbs on top. This dish can be served over cooked pasta or with toasted Italian bread.

Makes 6 servings.

Creamed Spinach

My grandmother used to make a dish similar to this recipe using pokeweed, which we called "poke salad." Pokeweed is in the greens family and usually grows wild in the spring. It is picked when the leaves are reddish green.

My grandmother always said, "You have to be careful with this wild green, because it will kill you." She was right; the berries and roots of pokeweed are poisonous. However, the shoots and leaves are safe to eat once they are par-boiled for about 10 to 15 minutes. Afterward, boil the pokeweed again with some salt pork or smoked turkey. Pokeweed tastes like spinach and is loaded with vitamins A and C. Some folks like to eat it with scrambled eggs.

If you come across some pokeweed, you can use it in this recipe instead of the spinach. Just remember to par-boil it first.

2 pounds fresh spinach	1 teaspoon chopped garlic
1 tablespoon olive oil	1 cup fresh corn kernels
2 tablespoons butter	1¼ cups half & half
2 cups chopped white button mushrooms	2 teaspoons freshly grated Parmesan (optional)

Cut the stems and roots of the spinach off and discard them. Place the spinach leaves in the kitchen sink, fill it with cool water, and let the spinach soak for about 5 minutes to let the dirt settle. Drain the sink, place the spinach in a colander, and wash the leaves under cool water. Once the spinach is clean, shake the leaves in the colander to remove excess water, then coarsely chop them and set aside. Heat the olive oil and butter in a large sauté pan or skillet for 2 minutes over high heat until hot (not smoky). Place the mushrooms and garlic in the pan and sauté them for about 2 to 3 minutes (be careful not to burn the garlic). Add the spinach and corn, cover the pan, and cook about 5 minutes. Pour in the half & half, cover and reduce the heat to low, and let simmer about 15 minutes or until the corn and mushrooms are tender, stirring every 2 minutes. Serve on a platter topped with Parmesan cheese. Can be eaten as a side dish or with fresh French or Italian bread.

Makes 6 servings.

Creamed Onions

If possible, use sweet onions for this recipe, like seasonal Vidalia, Maui, Valencia, or Bermuda.

⅓ cup vegetable oil
3 large sweet onions, peeled
   and cut into ½-inch slices
2 cups Mushroom Sauce, see
   recipe on page 132
¼ cup coarsely chopped
   capers

¼ teaspoon red cayenne
   pepper
¼ teaspoon dried oregano
salt and black pepper to taste
½ cup heavy cream

Heat a medium-size saucepan or skillet for about 1 minute over high heat until it is hot. Slowly add the oil and onions and cook for about 3 minutes, stirring constantly. Add the mushroom sauce, cover and reduce the heat to low, and cook about 5 minutes. Stir in the remainder of the ingredients, cover the pan again, and continue cooking for about 10 minutes or until the onions are tender. This dish can be served over cooked string beans or baked chicken.

Makes 4 to 6 servings.

Eggplant Tomato

In this eggplant recipe, I recommend drawing out the bitter juices. Cut the eggplant into slices, spread them out evenly, and sprinkle each side with salt. This also helps firm up the texture, so that the shape of the slice is held together during cooking. To prevent discoloration, soak the slices in salted water with some lemon juice.

1 large eggplant (about 1½ to 2 pounds)	2 cups whole milk
1 teaspoon salt	2½ cups vegetable oil
½ cup flour	3 cups coarsely chopped tomatoes
1 cup Italian seasoned bread crumbs	2 tablespoons chopped garlic
2 large eggs, lightly beaten	¼ cup freshly grated Parmesan cheese

Cut off the ends of the eggplant and trim off the outer skin. Cut into ¼-inch slices, sprinkle salt on each side, and let stand about 5 minutes. Rinse the slices with cool water, pat dry, and set aside. Combine the flour and bread crumbs together in a bowl and set aside. In a separate bowl, mix together the eggs and milk. Preheat the oil in a large frying pan over medium heat for about 2 minutes or until hot (but not smoky). Place the eggplant slices in the milk mixture, then dredge through the flour mixture. Fry the coated slices in the hot oil for about 1 minute on each side, then remove from the skillet and set aside. Pour out the oil, reserving the residue in the bottom of the skillet. Add the tomatoes and garlic to the skillet and cook constantly stirring about 3 minutes.

Return the cooked eggplant slices to the pan, sprinkle Parmesan cheese on top, cover and let cook about 20 minutes longer over low heat. Place the hot eggplant on a serving platter and sprinkle with more Parmesan cheese if desired. Serve immediately.

Makes 4 to 6 servings.

Green Beans with Onions and Bacon

When I was young, I enjoyed picking string beans from my mother's garden. They were so easy to pick — removing them from the vines required no effort. Mother would cook them with smoked turkey or pork parts.

This recipe can also be served as a chilled salad. Just drain the cooked liquid off and refrigerate 2 hours before serving.

1 pound fresh string beans
1 cup vegetable or chicken
   broth
12 pearl onions, cut
   lengthwise

salt and pepper to taste
6 strips cooked pork or
   turkey bacon, broken into
   small pieces

Wash the string beans in cool water, remove the ends, and break them into 1½-inch pieces; place them into a large saucepan. Add the vegetable broth, one cup of water, the onions, salt, and pepper to the pan. Cover the pan and cook over medium heat for 25 minutes or until the vegetables become soft. Place the vegetables on a platter and sprinkle with the bacon pieces.

Makes 6 servings.

Green Peas

This recipe calls for fresh green peas, which require a short amount of cooking time. If fresh green peas are not available, use frozen ones (place them in a colander and run cold water over them to remove the ice). I don't recommend using canned green peas—they are too salty and mushy.

4 cups fresh green peas (or 2   2 tablespoons butter
   16-oz frozen packages)   salt and pepper to taste
½ cup sliced water chestnuts

Place all the ingredients in a large saucepan or skillet, and add about 1 cup of water. Cover the pan and cook over low heat about 20 minutes or until the peas are tender.

Makes 4 to 6 servings.

Bell Peppers, Tomatoes and Mushrooms

When I studied at the Ecole de Gastronomique Francaise Ritz-Escoffier in Paris, I attended a lecture on sweet peppers. After the lecture, we spent a training session developing our tastebuds and learning how to distinguish the "sweet tasting" range of green, purple, red, orange, and yellow bell peppers. We had to learn this process blindfolded.

This dish can be served over cooked rice, grits, or grilled steak.

2 tablespoons vegetable oil

3 large green bell peppers, washed, ribs removed, and cut into ½-inch slices

1 large red bell pepper, washed, ribs removed, and cut into ½-inch slices

1 large yellow bell pepper, washed, ribs removed, and cut into ½-inch slices

2 cups coarsely chopped tomatoes

1 cup coarsely chopped white button mushrooms

½ teaspoon dried thyme

1 teaspoon garlic salt

½ teaspoon onion powder

1 teaspoon sugar

Preheat a large, heavy-bottomed skillet or saucepan over high heat for about 3 minutes. Slowly add the oil and bell peppers and sauté for about 5 minutes. Add the remaining ingredients, cover the skillet, reduce the heat to medium, and cook 20 minutes, stirring every 5 minutes.

Makes 6 servings.

Parmesan Leeks

Leeks are part of the onion family, have a very mild taste, and are used in many signature European dishes. However, leeks are hard to clean because dirt gets trapped between the layers of their skins. To clean them properly, I recommend the following: Trim off the top (leaving some of the green). Peel off and discard the outer leaves, which are usually very tough. Then trim the roots, split the leek into halves or quarters, and rinse the pieces in cold water to shake off any loose dirt.

2 tablespoon olive oil	½ cup dry white wine
1 pound leeks	½ cup freshly grated
3 large cucumbers, peeled, seeded, and cut lengthwise into thin 2-inch strips	Parmesan cheese

Heat the olive oil in a large saucepan or skillet over medium heat for about 1 minute until hot (not smoky). Add the leeks and cucumbers and sauté for about 5 minutes or until they are semi-soft. Pour in the wine, reduce the heat to low, cover the pan, and let simmer 12 to 15 minutes. Serve on a platter and sprinkle with Parmesan cheese.

Makes 4 to 6 servings.

Okra and Tomatoes

I like okra but, I did not enjoy picking it out of my mother's garden. In fact, none of the kids I grew up with enjoyed picking okra, because the skin can irritate you and make you feel itchy. As kids, we would pick vegetables while wearing summer clothes — short-sleeved shirts and shorts. It took me a long time to understand that experienced people always dressed in long-sleeved shirts and long pants when they picked vegetables from their gardens, to protect their skin from being exposed to itchy vegetables such as okra.

Okra is a wonderful vegetable. It tastes like asparagus, and it makes great soups and stews. Fried okra is also delicious, and is often served with a spicy relish such as chow chow.

1 pound fresh small okra pods	3 cups diced tomatoes
3 tablespoons olive oil	1 large onion, peeled and cut into ½-inch slices
2 tablespoons butter	salt and pepper to taste

Wash the okra and cut off the tops of the stems (do not cut into the pods). Heat the oil and butter in a large skillet or saucepan for about 2 minutes until hot. Add the okra and tomatoes, onion, salt, and pepper; cover the skillet and let simmer over medium heat about 20 minutes, stirring occasionally.

Makes 4 to 6 servings.

Pea and Carrot Croquettes

These vegetarian croquettes contain plenty of deep south flavor, especially when they are served with hot sauce.

2 cups cooked green peas	2 teaspoons Worcestershire sauce
1 cup cooked carrots	½ teaspoon salt
¼ cup sliced scallions	¼ teaspoon black pepper
2 large eggs	1 cup vegetable oil
½ cup plain bread crumbs, plus 1 cup	1 cup White Wine Sauce, see recipe on page 134
½ teaspoon ground cumin	
½ teaspoon garlic powder	

Combine the green peas, carrots, scallions, eggs, ½ cup bread crumbs, ground cumin, garlic powder, Worcestershire sauce, salt, and pepper in a food processor or a blender until coarsely mixed (not pureed). Pour 1 cup bread crumbs on a chopping board or flat surface. Shape the vegetable mixture into 4 to 6 patties, then coat each completely with bread crumbs and place them on a plate. Refrigerate them uncovered for 1 to 2 hours.

Heat the oil in a large frying pan over medium heat until hot. Add each patty and fry 2 to 3 minutes on each side or until light brown and firm. Set the cooked patties aside, pour the remainder of the oil out of the skillet, and pour in 1 cup of wine sauce. Cook over medium heat for about 2 minutes. Add the croquettes, cover, and cook about 2 minutes on each side. Serve hot.

Makes 4 to 6 patties.

Potato Croquettes and Gravy

Grandmother taught me that when a potato starts sprouting, that means it's getting old. She also told me to never put potato sprouts in my mouth because they are poisonous.

One day, I was visiting my Aunt Carrie, who at the time lived about 10 miles from Clarksdale. In her kitchen, I saw a 10-pound unopened bag of white potatoes that had sprouts on them, so I told her that she should throw them away. She told me that the sprouts are good for planting more potatoes in her garden. At that moment, I realized that I had much to learn.

I cook these potato croquettes with a brown sauce. However, the Mushroom Sauce on page 132, Herbal Sauce on page 131, or Dill Sauce on pages 131–32 can also be used.

2 cups white potatoes, peeled and boiled	2 large eggs, lightly beaten
1 cup diced onions	salt and pepper to taste
½ cup diced sweet red bell peppers	¾ cup plain bread crumbs
½ cup diced sweet green bell peppers	nonstick cooking spray
	1 cup vegetable oil
	2 cups Brown Sauce, see recipe on page 128

Place the cooked white potatoes in a large mixing bowl and coarsely mash them with a potato masher, retaining some of the lumps. Add the onions, red and green bell peppers, eggs, salt, black pepper, and bread crumbs; stir together with a large spoon. Shape the potato mixture into 4 to 6 croquettes and spray each one completely with nonstick cooking spray, then place them in the refrigerator for 1 to 2 hours.

Heat the oil in a large skillet or saucepan over medium heat for about 2 minutes until hot. Fry each croquette about 3 to 4 minutes on each side or until they turn light brown and firm. Remove the croquettes from the pan and set aside. Pour out the remaining oil and wipe the skillet with a clean towel. Place 2 cups of brown sauce in the skillet and cook over medium heat about 2 minutes or until hot, stirring constantly. Return the croquettes to the skillet, cover, and let them cook about 3 minutes on each side.

Makes 4 to 6 croquettes.

Potato Dumplings

My grandmother perfected her recipe for gnocchi (Italian potato dumplings). She learned it from the Italian family that she worked for as a cook for forty years. Grandmother served gnocchi with a homemade marinara sauce, always topped with a high-quality Parmigiano-Reggiano.

This recipe for potato dumplings is my modified, simpler version of gnocchi. They can be made in advance and frozen for later use.

2 large baking potatoes
(about 1 pound)
1 large egg, beaten
½ cup all purpose flour
½ teaspoon salt
¼ teaspoon freshly grated
nutmeg

¼ teaspoon black pepper
¼ cup freshly grated
Parmigiano-Reggiano
cheese
3 cups Tomato Sauce, see
page 133

Place the potatoes in a large pot of water and boil them over medium heat for about 35 minutes or until they are easily pierced with a fork. Cool the potatoes in cold water, peel them, and press them through a potato ricer or coarse sieve. Set aside. In a medium-size mixing bowl, pour in the beaten egg, and set aside. Mix together the flour, salt, nutmeg, pepper, cheese, then add to the beaten egg. Fold in the mashed potatoes and mix well. Dust your hands with flour and divide the potato mixture into 4 equal parts. Roll each section into a rope shape about ½-inch thick. Cut the rope shape into ½-inch nuggets. Take each piece and roll it along the inside of a dinner fork (pressing the opposite side gently with your thumb). The finished potato dumplings should have an oval shape with the ridges on one side and an indentation on the other side.

Once the dumplings are formed, place them on a large baking sheet lined with a floured kitchen towel. At this stage, the dumplings can either be cooked or stored frozen for later use.

Bring 4 quarts of water to boil over high heat, then reduce to medium. Drop about half of the dumplings into the water and cook them for about 1 minute or until they rise to the surface. If they are frozen cook them 3 to 4 minutes.

Meanwhile, heat 3 cups of tomato sauce in a large saucepan over medium heat 3 minutes or until hot. Gently add the cooked potato dumplings to the tomato sauce, cover the pan with a lid, and let simmer about 2 to 3 minutes (be careful not to overcook).

Makes 4 servings.

Red Cabbage and Chestnuts

I remember going grocery shopping with my mother when I was about ten years old. I wanted her to buy a red cabbage instead of the typical green cabbage that she always bought. Mother asked me if I was *crazy*—she told me that red cabbage costs twice as much as the green ones. She also said the red ones become sweeter when you cook them, so they don't smother as well as the green ones, and they also take longer to cook. She was right on all points. Mother told me that red cabbage tastes great, in cold salads or sautéed with mushrooms and onions.

I made this recipe of Red Cabbage and Chestnuts for some of my friends, and it was an instant hit. The chestnuts complement the sweet and tangy flavor of the red cabbage. This recipe can also be enjoyed during the holiday season, Thanksgiving through New Year's Day.

2 pounds red cabbage, washed and shredded	½ cup cider vinegar
½ pound sliced white button mushrooms	½ teaspoon white pepper
1½ cups commercial precooked sliced chestnuts	½ cup coarsely chopped walnuts
	½ cup dark raisins
	½ cup yellow raisins

Place a large saucepan or Dutch oven on the stove and add all the ingredients except the nuts and raisins. Add about 2 cups water to the pan, cover with a lid, and cook over medium heat about 40 minutes, stirring occasionally. Add the nuts and raisins and continue to cook about 15 minutes longer or until the cabbage is tender.

Makes 6 to 8 servings.

Succotash

Succotash is one of those melting pot dishes (influenced by Native American, African, and European cuisine) that was considered a stew and served as a one-pot meal in many parts of the south. But as years passed, many folks began serving succotash as a condiment or side dish along with black-eyed peas, fried fish, baked chicken, barbecue ribs, or smothered pork chops.

I like to serve succotash over a big bowl of buttered grits or stir some in my cornbread batter before baking.

½ cup butter
2 cups diced onions
1 cup diced sweet yellow bell
    peppers
1 cup diced sweet green bell
    peppers

3 cups frozen lima beans
4 cups fresh or frozen corn
    kernels
2 cups diced tomatoes
1 teaspoon sugar
salt and black pepper to taste

Melt the butter in a large skillet or saucepan over medium heat. Add the onions and sauté for about 2 minutes or until they turn translucent. Add the remaining ingredients, cover, reduce the heat to low, and cook about 15 to 20 minutes or until the vegetables are tender.

Makes 6 servings.

Boston Lettuce

Butterhead or any mild-flavored, soft leaf lettuce can be used instead of Boston. I like serving this as a side dish, with pot roast and potatoes.

½ cup butter
10 small heads Boston lettuce, rinsed torn into large pieces and drained in a colander
1½ cups vegetable or chicken broth

1 tablespoon freshly squeezed lemon juice
½ teaspoon salt
½ teaspoon white pepper
3 strips bacon, cooked and broken into small pieces (optional)

Heat the butter in a large frying pan or saucepan over medium heat until melted, but not browned. Add the lettuce and cook about 10 minutes, stirring frequently. Add the remaining ingredients except the bacon, reduce the heat to low, cover the frying pan, and cook 15 minutes or until the lettuce is very tender. Remove the lid from the pan, turn the heat to high, and cook off the liquid. Pour on a serving platter and sprinkle bacon pieces on top.

Makes 4 to 6 servings.

2

Fish and Seafood

About Fish and Seafood

ONE OF MY FAVORITE FISH recipes that my grandmother would prepare was a buffalo fish stew. She would make it with corn, butter beans, onions, tomatoes, buffalo fish steaks, salt, and pepper. The stew would simmer over a low flame about 1 hour. Once it was cooked, she would ladle some in a large bowl for my grandfather. Even before tasting it, he would put plenty of hot sauce in it. Granddaddy loved fiery hot, spicy food.

I loved this dish. Grandmother would sometimes serve it with some scalloped potatoes or long-grain white rice. Sometimes she made this fish stew using catfish, which was easier to eat because it contained far fewer bones than buffalo fish, but it tasted less authentic.

Both Grandmother and Mother would purchase fish either from the local fisherman, who caught them in wild lakes and rivers, or from the grocery store. Sometimes Mother would go fishing on the local fish farms that sprouted up across Mississippi during the 1970s.

We bought other kinds of seafood from the larger supermarkets, whose buyers would have a distributor routinely ship freshly caught crawfish, shrimp, and crabs from the Mississippi Gulf coast.

Here's a checklist that can be used as a guide when buying fresh fish and seafood.

1. Do not buy fish if the eyes are dull, gray, or cloudy. They should be moist, clear, and bright.
2. Do not buy fish if the gills are dull and gray. They should be pinkish or bright red.
3. Fresh fish should smell like the sea, and the flesh should spring back if you press it.
4. Clams, mussels, and oysters should be tightly closed when you buy them. They should smell like fresh seafood. If they smell like ammonia, they are probably spoiled. Once they are cooked, they should open. If not, discard them.
5. If possible, try to buy medium-, large-, and jumbo-size shrimp with their heads and tails attached—they taste even fresher when they are purchased this way. Cleaning and deveining them at home can be a little time-consuming, but it's worth it.

Selecting and Storing Fish and Seafood

If you buy fish and seafood from the supermarket, where it's displayed behind a glass case, ask the purveyor how old it is and how many more days are left before it's no longer fresh.

Try keeping your fish and seafood close to 32 degrees F in the refrigerator. This low temperature will keep your fish fresh for a couple of days. Keep in mind that most American refrigerators are preset to 37 degrees F. If you plan to use the fish or seafood within one or two days, place it in a container and put ice cubes over the fish or seafood until ready to use. If you don't plan to use your fish or seafood within two days, it is best to freeze it. Be sure to thaw it thoroughly before using.

Barbecued Shrimp

About twenty years ago, I had my first meal of authentic barbecued shrimp, prepared for me by one of my friends, who was a local chef in New Orleans. He cooked large shrimp with their shells on and their heads and tails still attached—and the shrimp were not deveined. He told me that once the shrimp is served on the table, everyone can peel their own. I also noticed that my friend didn't use any barbecue sauce. This is a dish that is eaten with your fingers, and the name Barbecued Shrimp is all about flavor, not a bottle of commercial barbecue sauce from the grocery market.

I like serving this barbecued shrimp recipe with some French bread so that it can be dipped in the reserved juices from the cooked shrimp.

1 cup unsalted butter	2 teaspoons Worcestershire
2 tablespoons freshly	sauce
chopped garlic	¼ teaspoon cayenne pepper
1 tablespoon fresh oregano	½ cup seafood stock or
(or 1 teaspoon dried)	vegetable broth
1 tablespoon fresh marjoram	½ cup dry white wine
(or 1 teaspoon dried)	
1 pound large shrimp, washed	
(unpeeled, with head,	
tails, and legs attached)	

Melt the butter in a large skillet over medium heat. Add the garlic, oregano, and marjoram, and cook about 3 minutes. Add the remainder of the ingredients, cover, and cook about 3 to 5 minutes or until the shrimp turns pink.

Makes 4 servings.

Catfish Steaks with Lemon Pepper Sauce

Catfish is very popular these days. Residents as far away as California are eating three times the amount of catfish compared to ten years ago, when it was still considered a regional fish eaten mostly in the south and midwestern parts of the country.

The Catfish Institute (a Mississippi-based association of catfish farmers, processors, and feed manufacturers), has taken this once muddy-tasting, garbage-labeled fish to new heights in terms of flavor and overall quality. Farm-raised catfish has a fresher taste, and doesn't have a fishy smell. Many chefs and restaurateurs have given their seal of approval by using only farm-raised catfish. And because of the greater demand for farm-raised catfish, many farmers throughout the south have replaced their cotton, soybean, and peanut fields with catfish farms.

1 tablespoon vegetable oil	⅓ cup melted butter
½ cup diced red bell peppers	1 tablespoon lemon pepper
½ cup diced yellow bell	seasoning
peppers	4 4-ounce catfish steaks
2 cups diced white potatoes,	½ lemon, cut into 4 wedges
peeled	(for garnishing)
½ cup dry white wine	

Heat the vegetable oil in a large skillet or saucepan over medium heat for about 2 minutes or until hot. Add the red and yellow bell peppers and potatoes, and sauté about 2 minutes or until soft. Pour in the wine and butter and cook 3 minutes longer. Sprinkle the lemon pepper seasoning on both sides of the catfish steaks and put them in the skillet. Cover and simmer about 8 to 10 minutes on each side. Garnish with lemon wedges.

Makes 4 servings.

Cajun Salmon

Catfish can be substituted for the salmon used in this recipe, and the Creole Sauce recipe on page 130 can be used as an alternative sauce.

4 6-ounce salmon fillets, skin removed
2 tablespoons commercial Cajun seasoning
½ cup melted butter
1 cup seafood stock or chicken broth

½ teaspoon dried thyme
2 tablespoons freshly chopped parsley, for garnish

Rinse the salmon fillets under cold water and pat dry with paper towels. Rub some commercial Cajun seasoning on both sides of each fillet, and set aside. Heat a large, heavy-bottomed skillet over medium heat. Melt the butter (don't burn it), put the fillets in the skillet, and cook about 1 minute on each side. Add the remaining ingredients and cover the skillet, reduce the heat to low, and let simmer about 5 minutes. Use a large spatula to turn the fillets, and cook uncovered about 4 to 5 minutes or until the salmon is pink. Assemble the fillets on a serving platter, sprinkle with parsley, and serve.

Makes 4 servings.

Crawfish Étoufée

Whenever I'm in my kitchen cooking Cajun or Creole foods, I automatically think about my friend the late Jamie Shannon, who was the executive chef at Commander's Palace in New Orleans for over seventeen years. This is the restaurant that made both Paul Prudhomme and Emeril Lagasse celebrity chefs. Jamie was next in line to become the big celebrity chef out of New Orleans. He had won a James Beard Award and made many, many appearances on the Food Network and national news programs.

Jamie and I had many conversations about the differences and similarities between Cajun and Creole cooking. Both of us thought that Crawfish Étoufée was somewhere in the middle, influenced by both of these rich culinary histories. Sadly, Jamie died of cancer in 2001.

5 pounds crawfish (live if possible)

4 tablespoons peanut butter brown roux (see recipe below)

1 cup chopped onions

1 cup chopped celery

2 cups seafood stock or vegetable broth

1 tablespoon chopped garlic

4 cups freshly chopped tomatoes

1 tablespoon Worcestershire sauce

¼ teaspoon cayenne pepper

¼ teaspoon freshly ground black pepper

1½ teaspoons salt

Soak the crawfish in cold water for about 10 minutes, then wash them thoroughly under cold running water. Boil 4 quarts of water in an 8- to 10-quart heavy pot or Dutch oven. Using tongs, drop in the crawfish and boil them quickly, uncovered, about 5 minutes. Drain the crawfish in a large colander. When cool, peel them (with your hands, break off the ridged tails, snap them in half lengthwise and remove the meat in one piece. If you like, you can snap off the large claws, break them with a nutcracker, and pick out the claw meat). Place all the crawfish meat (should yield about 2¼ cups) in a small bowl and set aside. Discard the shells, heads, and intestinal matter.

Heat the roux in a large pot over medium heat until it has melted. Add the onions and celery and sauté about 5 minutes or until they are soft. Stir in the seafood stock, garlic, tomatoes, Worcestershire sauce, cayenne pepper, black pepper, and salt, reduce the heat to low, and cook about 25 minutes. Stir in the crawfish meat and heat through, about 2 minutes. Serve over cooked long-grain white rice or pasta.

Roux Ingredients and Instructions

1 cup vegetable oil   1 cup all-purpose flour

Pour the oil in a medium-size heavy bottomed skillet over medium heat until hot, about 3 minutes. Add the flour and stir constantly with a wooden spoon or a whisk until it reaches the desired color. Cook 5 minutes for light brown, 10 minutes for peanut butter brown, 15 minutes for dark nutty brown, 25 to 30 minutes for black.

Note: Roux is a crucial ingredient used in many Cajun and Creole dishes. It's a thickening and flavoring agent that needs to be cooked slowly and with constant attention.

Makes 6 to 8 servings.

Creamed Clams

Fresh clams are still a little challenging to buy in this country unless you live along the east or west coast. If you can't find fresh clams, canned ones work just as well in this recipe.

2 tablespoons olive oil
1 cup chopped onions
3 tablespoons freshly
   chopped garlic
1 tablespoon freshly squeezed
   lemon juice

2 pounds fresh clams, cleaned
   and removed from the
   shell (or 2 10-oz cans,
   drained)
2 cups heavy cream
¼ teaspoon crushed red
   pepper flakes
salt and black pepper to taste

Heat the olive oil in a large sauté pan over medium heat about 1 minute until hot. Add the onions and garlic and sauté until the onions turn soft. Add the lemon juice and cook about 2 minutes. Roughly chop the clams and add them to the pan along with the cream, red pepper, salt, and black pepper. Reduce the heat to low, cover, and let simmer 5 to 6 minutes. This dish can be served on top of cooked pasta or vegetables such as asparagus or broccoli.

Makes 4 to 6 servings.

Flounder Florentine

Flounder is a mild-flavored flatfish found in the coastal waters of the Atlantic Ocean. It has a brownish-gray skin, and its flesh is pinkish-white. To save some preparation time, have your fish provider at the market clean and cut your fish into steaks.

1 tablespoon unsalted butter
4 tablespoons flour
½ teaspoon salt
2 cups half & half
2 pounds fresh spinach, washed, drained and coarsely chopped
2 cups Celery Sauce, see recipe on page 129

3 large eggs, lightly beaten
3 tablespoons finely chopped shallots
salt and black pepper to taste
2 pounds flounder, cleaned and cut into steaks (about 4 to 6 pieces)

Heat the butter in a small saucepan or sauté pan over medium heat until it melts. Whisk in the flour and ½ teaspoon salt. Then, gradually whisk in the half & half, continuing to whisk until it comes to a boil. Remove from heat. Place the spinach in large skillet or sauté pan with ½ cup water, cover, and cook over medium heat about 5 minutes. Whisk the egg into the cooled flour base, then add it to the spinach mixture, add the shallots, cover, and let cook about 3 minutes. Add the flounder steaks, cover, reduce the heat to low, and let simmer about 15 minutes or until the fish is slightly firm and flaky.

Makes 4 to 6 servings.

Fricassee of Clams

Even though *fricassee* is a French term that refers to a stew made with a white sauce, sometimes I like to make this recipe with Creole Sauce (recipe on page 130), which is a tomato-based sauce.

2 tablespoons olive oil
1 cup diced yellow bell
    peppers
1 cup diced onions
2 pounds freshly cleaned
    clams, coarsely chopped
    (or 2 16-ounce cans,
    drained)

2 cups heavy cream
1 tablespoon fresh tarragon
    (or 1 teaspoon dried)
1 tablespoon fresh thyme (or
    1 teaspoon dried)
salt and black pepper to taste

Heat the olive oil in a large skillet over medium heat for 2 minutes or until hot. Add the yellow bell peppers and onions and sauté about 2 minutes until they are semi-soft. Add the clams, cream, tarragon, thyme, salt, and pepper, cover with lid, and cook about 5 to 6 minutes. Serve over roasted white potato wedges or french fries.

Makes 6 servings.

Low Country Shrimp and Rice

Low Country often refers to the region located in the southeast part of South Carolina, which extends to the coastal islands along the ocean, including popular islands such as Hilton Head and Hunting Island. The foods of Low Country are just as interesting as its history. Like Louisiana's melting pot of cuisine, Low Country cooking is a mixture of African, European, and Native American influences.

The popular Low Country shrimp and grits is a classical signature dish that's eaten anytime of the day in this area. I use rice instead of grits in this recipe. Rice was an important commodity in the Carolinas, including Low Country. In fact, many of the locals in Low Country still call rice "Carolina's Gold." That name came from the antebellum area (pre–Civil War), when many plantation owners become very wealthy from rice harvesting. Many historians believe West African slaves brought their knowledge of rice harvesting to South Carolina—turning the marshes into rice fields.

4 slices bacon, diced
1 cup diced onions
2 tablespoons garlic chopped fine
2 pounds medium shrimp (about 40), peeled, deveined, with shells, heads, tails, and legs removed
1½ cups long-grain white rice

2¼ cups shrimp stock or water
3 slices American cheese, cut into small pieces

Shrimp stock:
⅓ cup dry white wine
2 cups shrimp shells
½ cup chopped carrots
½ cup chopped onions
1 quart water

Place all the shrimp stock ingredients into a 3- or 4-quart pot and let simmer over medium heat for about 30 minutes. Set aside.

Cook the diced bacon in a large skillet over medium heat until the pieces are crisp, but not burned. Add the onions and garlic and sauté for about 2 minutes. Add the shrimp and ¼ cup shrimp stock, cover, and let simmer about 2 minutes or until the shrimp turn pink. Set aside.

Pour the rice and the remainder of the shrimp stock into a

medium saucepan and bring to a boil over high heat. Reduce the heat to low, cover, and cook the rice about 18 to 20 minutes or until it becomes tender and all the stock is absorbed. Add the cheese and stir until it has melted. Spoon the shrimp over the rice.

Makes 4 to 6 servings.

Provençal Oysters

Whenever I visit my adopted French family, the Dauliacs, who live in the Brittany countryside of France along the shore of the Atlantic Ocean, we always stop in the early afternoon where the fishermen work to have some fresh raw oysters. I usually bring my Tabasco pepper sauce and fresh lemons, and the Dauliac family would always bring a couple of bottles of good white wine. We would enjoy a wonderful feast for a couple of hours, then travel back to the house and start making plans for the next meal, later that evening.

This recipe calls for the oysters to be cooked, which gives them the tasty southwestern French flavor of Provence.

2 tablespoons olive oil
2 tablespoons freshly
    chopped garlic
1 tablespoon fresh rosemary
    (or 1 teaspoon dried)
1 tablespoon fresh thyme (or
    1 teaspoon dried)
1 tablespoon freshly chopped
    chives (or 1 teaspoon
    dried)

½ cup black olives, pitted,
    and coarsely chopped
½ cup dry white wine
2 pounds fresh oysters,
    cleaned and removed
    from the shell

Heat the olive oil in a large sauté pan or skillet over medium heat for 1 minute or until hot. Sauté the garlic until it starts to turn light brown (but don't burn it). Add the rosemary, thyme, chives, olives, and sauté for about 2 minutes. Pour in the wine and oysters, cover, and let simmer about 3 to 5 minutes. Pour the cooked oysters and the sauce into a serving bowl and serve with fresh bread or cornbread.

Makes 4 to 6 servings.

Red Snapper with Sherry Sauce

Typical recipes using red snapper usually call for it to be steamed or baked and served in some type of savory sauce with vegetables on the side. This recipe uses a sherry sauce. Serve over Buttered Kale, see recipe on page 20.

2 pounds red snapper fillets	2 tablespoons lemon juice
¼ cup melted butter	¼ teaspoon ground allspice
1 teaspoon garlic powder	2 bay leaves
1 cup diced onions	1 cup dry sherry

Cut the fillets into 4 1-inch pieces and cover each piece with melted butter, then sprinkle garlic powder all over them. Pour the remainder of the butter into a large skillet, add the onions, and sauté until they become soft. Add the lemon juice, allspice, bay leaves, and sherry, cover, and let cook about 3 minutes. Add the fish fillets, cover again, and let simmer for 6 to 7 minutes on each side. Remove the bay leaves and serve.

Makes 4 to 6 servings.

Lobster and Saffron Rice

Fresh or canned crabmeat can be substituted for the fresh lobster used in this recipe. If using canned crabmeat, drain the juice before adding it to the rest of the ingredients.

Saffron is still considered the most expensive spice on earth; it can easily cost hundreds of dollars per pound. I purchase my saffron at ethnic grocery stores such as Asian and Mid-Eastern, where it's usually much cheaper than at large grocery stores or upscale gourmet markets.

2 tablespoons bottled-garlic flavored oil
¼ cup fresh finely chopped parsley
2 tablespoons finely chopped shallots
1 pound fresh lobster meat, coarsely chopped

1 cup long-grain white rice
½ teaspoon saffron
½ teaspoon salt
½ cup raisins
1 lemon, sliced into wedges for garnish

Place the garlic oil in a medium-size skillet and heat over high heat for 1 minute or until it turns hot. Add the parsley and shallots and sauté about 30 seconds, reduce the heat to low, and add the lobster. Cover the skillet and let simmer 3 to 4 minutes or until the lobster meat is semi-firm, but not tough. Pour the cooked lobster meat and its juices into a bowl and set aside.

Pour 2 cups of water into a medium-size pot and bring to boil over high heat. Add the rice, salt, saffron, and raisins; cover, reduce the heat to low, and cook about 20 minutes or until the rice grains are soft and the liquid is absorbed. Serve the cooked lobster over the rice and garnish with lemon wedges.

Makes 4 servings.

Salmon Steaks

Back in May 2002, I went to Fairbanks, Alaska, to visit my good friend Deon Williams, who at the time was stationed there by the United States military. On Deon's downtime, we visited a place called Santa's Smokehouse (a retail store), which had some of the best smoked salmon that I've ever tasted. The owner of the business told me that he uses king salmon caught in the Yukon River, which is said to have the highest omega-3 fatty acid content of any salmon in the world. If you're ever in that neck of the woods, Santa's Smokehouse is well worth the trip.

In this smothered version of fresh salmon steaks, I use dried herbs and tomato sauce to create a lot of flavor. If you have smoked salmon available, you can use it in this recipe. Just add the dry herbs to the tomato sauce, and let the smoked salmon simmer in the tomato sauce about 15 to 20 minutes, or until it's tender.

1 teaspoon dried oregano
1 teaspoon dried thyme
1 teaspoon sweet paprika
½ teaspoon salt (skip if you are using smoked salmon)
⅓ cup vegetable oil (skip if you are using smoked salmon)

4 4-ounce salmon steaks
nonstick cooking spray (skip if you are using smoked salmon)
2 cups tomato sauce, see recipe on page 133

Combine the oregano, thyme, paprika, salt, and vegetable oil in a small bowl and mix well with a spoon. Rub the mixture on both sides of the salmon steaks and set aside. Spray some nonstick cooking spray in a large skillet, then heat over medium heat. Once the spray is hot, or turns slightly brown put the steaks in the skillet and cook about 3 minutes on each side. Pour in the tomato sauce, reduce the heat to low, cover, and let simmer about 10 minutes or until the salmon is cooked.

Makes 4 servings.

Scallops

When I was young, I had no idea that scallops, like clams and oysters, were encased in shells. This is because they were always removed from their shells before they arrived at the fish markets or grocery stores. The only seafood that we had regularly in Clarksdale were shrimp and crabs. Scallops were very expensive and rarely available fresh in the stores.

2 tablespoons butter	¼ teaspoon paprika
1 tablespoon flour	½ teaspoon garlic powder
1 cup half & half	1 pound scallops, washed
½ teaspoon salt	

Melt the butter in a medium-size saucepan over low heat. Add the flour and stir until a grainy sauce forms. Gradually pour in the half & half and continue to stir until the sauce is smooth. Sprinkle in the salt, paprika, and garlic powder, and pour in the scallops; cover and let simmer about 10 to 12 minutes. Serve over cooked pasta with fresh grated Parmesan cheese.

Makes 4 servings.

Shrimp Creole

A few years ago, I stopped by my friend Leah Chase's restaurant Dooky Chase in New Orleans. Leah's restaurant has been open for over 55 years. She was still working long hours there, seven days a week. A few hours before I stopped in to see her, she had just prepared a luncheon for one hundred doctors, who took a break from their convention in the Big Easy to enjoy Leah's delicious meals.

I couldn't wait to see what Leah was going to make for my lunch. She made me one of her specialties, Shrimp Creole, and the tomatoes that she used in her recipe tasted so sweet and natural. She told me that they were Creole tomatoes, grown in the fields locally. "It's in the rich dirt here, thanks to the Mississippi River. Creole tomatoes grown here are picked when they are ripe on the vine, not early like the ones sold in the supermarkets across the country," she said. I learned from Leah that when making Shrimp Creole, using good-quality tomatoes is just as important as using good-quality shrimp. Sadly, Dooky Chase is closed due to the 2005 hurricane Katrina disaster.

½ cup unsalted butter
2 cups coarsely chopped
    onions
2 cups coarsely chopped
    green bell peppers
1 cup coarsely chopped celery
1 bay leaf
1 tablespoon sweet paprika
3½ cups freshly chopped ripe
    tomatoes

1 cup tomato juice
½ cup Worcestershire sauce
4 dashes Tabasco sauce
    (optional)
salt and black pepper to taste
3 pounds fresh raw shrimp,
    peeled, deveined, with
    heads, tails, and legs
    removed

Melt the butter in a large, heavy-bottomed skillet or Dutch oven over medium heat. Add the chopped onions, green peppers, and celery and sauté about 3 minutes or until soft. Add the bayleaf, sprinkle in the paprika, and add the chopped tomatoes, tomato juice, and Worcestershire sauce; cover and let cook about 2 to 3 minutes. Sprinkle in the Tabasco sauce, add the salt, black pepper, and the shrimp, cover, and cook about 10 minutes or until the shrimp turn pink. Serve over cooked long-grain white rice.

Makes 6 to 8 servings.

Shrimp, Eggs, and Gravy (Brown Sauce)

This recipe is usually served for breakfast or Sunday brunch. However, I've served it for dinner, along with mashed potatoes or sautéed squash.

2 large eggs, lightly beaten
2 large carrots, peeled and shredded
¼ cup heavy cream
½ cup scallions
1 cup diced tomatoes
2 tablespoons butter

½ pound medium shrimp, peeled, deveined, with head, tails, and legs removed
1 cup Brown Sauce, see recipe on page 128

Add the eggs, shredded carrots, cream, scallions, and diced tomatoes to a medium-size mixing bowl and whisk together until well combined. Melt the butter in a large skillet over medium heat. Pour in the egg mixture and scramble until cooked. Add the shrimp and gravy and reduce the heat to low, cover the skillet, and cook for about 5 minutes. Serve on a platter along with some biscuits or rolls.

Makes 6 servings.

Shrimp and Red Rice

I was about twenty-two years old when I first had red rice, at a small restaurant in downtown Charleston, South Carolina. A couple sitting next to me ordered red rice as a side dish. When I first saw it, I thought it was some type of sweet rice pudding. But I quickly learned that red rice is a savory dish that's usually cooked with fresh tomatoes and seasonal vegetables.

This recipe is my version of red rice, made with fresh shrimp to give it that signature Low Country flavor.

1 pound medium shrimp,
    peeled, deveined, with
    heads, tails, and legs
    removed
¼ cup vegetable oil
½ cup diced onions
½ cup diced sweet green bell
    peppers

2 tablespoons tomato paste
1 cup diced tomatoes
2 cups long-grain white rice
½ teaspoon salt
½ cup water

Chop the shrimp coarsely and set aside. Pour the oil in a large skillet or sauté pan over medium heat for 2 minutes until hot. Add the onions and green bell peppers and sauté until soft. Add the tomato paste and diced tomatoes, cover the skillet, reduce the heat to low, and let simmer about 15 minutes, stirring about every 2 minutes. Turn the heat off and set the skillet aside.

Bring about 4 cups of water to boil in a medium-size pot. Stir in the rice and salt. Reduce the heat to low, cover, and let cook about 20 minutes or until the rice grains become soft and all the liquid has been absorbed.

Heat the large skillet containing the vegetables over medium heat for 3 minutes or until hot. Stir in the coarsely chopped shrimp, cover, and let simmer about 4 to 5 minutes. Stir in the cooked rice and cook about 2 to 3 minutes longer.

Makes 6 servings.

Skillet Tuna Casserole

I recommend using oil-packed tuna for this recipe because it has a richer taste compared to tuna packed in water. If desired, canned salmon can be substituted for the tuna. Just remember to drain the juice and remove the bones.

2 6½-ounce cans tuna (oil packed)

4 cups cooked macaroni pasta

1 8-ounce can mushroom soup

½ cup evaporated milk

½ cup finely chopped onions

1½ cups grated Parmesan cheese

1 cup Italian seasoned bread crumbs

Combine the tuna, pasta, mushroom soup, milk, and onions in a large skillet. Add ½ cup of water, turn the heat to medium, cover, and let cook about 10 minutes, stirring occasionally. Sprinkle in the Parmesan cheese and cook about 3 to 5 minutes. If all the liquid has absorbed, add a little more milk. Sprinkle the bread crumbs on top and place the skillet under the broiler for 3 to 4 minutes or until the bread crumbs turn brown.

Makes 6 to 8 servings.

Sole in White Wine Sauce

This recipe calls for sole, but any firm-fleshed flatfish such as plaice, flounder, or turbot can be used. If possible, have the fish cut into fillet pieces at the fish market or grocery store.

1 tablespoon olive oil
1 tablespoon butter
4 6-ounce sole fillets
¼ teaspoon ground allspice
salt and black pepper to taste

2 cups White Wine Sauce, see
recipe on page 134
4 carrots, peeled and
shredded

Place the olive oil and butter in a large skillet or saucepan over medium heat until the butter is melted. Put the fillets in the skillet and brown about 2 minutes on each side. Sprinkle in the ground allspice, salt, and pepper. Pour in the wine sauce, cover the skillet, and let simmer 6 to 8 minutes. Turn the fillets over, add the shredded carrots, and cook 6 to 8 minutes longer or until the fish is firm and slightly flaky.

Makes 4 servings.

Tomato Parmesan Sea Bass

I use sea bass fillets in this recipe because they are easier to serve, but cooking the whole fish with the head attached can be nice and makes a wonderful presentation. If you decide to cook the whole sea bass, be sure to add extra cooking time, about 5 minutes per extra pound.

⅓ cup olive oil

1 tablespoon chopped garlic

1 cup coarsely chopped
onions

½ cup pitted black olives,
coarsely chopped

2 pounds sea bass fillets (6 to
8 pieces)

2½ cups Tomato Sauce, see
recipe on page 133

½ cup freshly grated
Parmesan cheese

Heat the oil over medium heat in a large, heavy-bottomed skillet for 2 minutes or until hot. Add the garlic and onions and cook until the onions turn soft. Add the olives and cook about 2 minutes. Add the fillets and tomato sauce, cover the skillet, and let simmer about 7 to 8 minutes on each side. Sprinkle in the Parmesan cheese.

Makes 6 to 8 servings.

Trout and Potatoes

If you ever have the chance to go to Hot Springs, Virginia, be sure to have the signature trout meal at the renowned Homestead Resort. Sautéed Mountain Trout Homestead has been a favorite for many years there. The trout is caught locally in the nearby Allegheny streams. The chef at the Homestead cooks it in butter, parsley, grapes, and almonds.

Here's my adapted version, served with potatoes.

2 1-pound whole trout

2 tablespoons freshly
chopped parsley

½ teaspoon salt

½ teaspoon black pepper

1 tablespoon peanut oil

2 tablespoons butter

½ cup Dill Sauce, see recipe
on page 131

½ pound baking potatoes
(about 2 to 3)

Clean the trout and butterfly them. (Cut lengthwise, down the belly, leaving the backbone attached and keeping the skin on—but scales removed.) Season the trout with parsley, salt, and pepper; set aside.

Place the peanut oil and butter in a large frying pan over high heat until hot. Place the seasoned trout in the hot pan, reduce the heat to low, and let cook 8 to 10 minutes on each side. Add ½ cup dill sauce to the pan, cover and cook about 5 minutes.

Meanwhile, wash and scrub the baking potatoes. Pierce them a few times with a sharp knife and microwave them on high, 5 to 6 minutes or until they can be easily pierced with a fork. Remove them from the microwave and let rest about 1 minute. Slice the potatoes in half lengthwise, season with salt and pepper, and serve with the trout.

Makes 4 to 6 servings.

3

Meats, Poultry, and Game

About Meat, Poultry and Game

MOST OF MY FRIENDS know how much I enjoy talking about the time I spent attending cooking school at the Ecole de Gastronomique Francaise Ritz-Escoffier in Paris. They've heard about how much I loved shopping at the wonderful meat, poultry, and game markets. These markets would display their merchandise just like fine clothing and jewelry in the haute couture shops in Paris.

The first time I saw a whole chicken with its head and feet attached at these markets, I was amazed because I thought only folks from the deep southern part of the United States could stand such a sight. The whole chickens were displayed on a bed of crushed ice, and each one was stamped with a serial number that provided the age of the chicken, the weight, name of business, the date it was killed, and a freshness date. It was also at these wonderful markets that I first discovered how expensive good-quality foods can be. But they're worth it because of the quality and taste.

Large grocery stores are not the norm in Paris. The Parisians prefer shopping at specialty shops such as cheese shops, bread and pastry shops, meat, poultry, and game shops, chocolate shops, and vegetable markets. One of my good Parisian friends with whom I love to shop told me, "Our food shops are just as important as our fashion houses."

Here's a useful checklist for selecting meats, poultry, and game:

1. There are eight USDA grades for selecting beef: prime, choice, select, standard, commercial, utility, cutter and canner. These selections are determined by the shape of the meat, ratio of fat to lean meat, ratio of meat to bones, color, and marbling of lean flesh.
2. There are four USDA grades for selecting lamb: prime, choice, good, or utility.
3. Pork is graded on a rarely used number system: 1, 2, or 3.
4. Poultry is graded on a letter system: A, B, or C. Grading is determined by the shape of the bird; ratio of meat to bone; the absence of pin feathers, hair, and down; and the number of tears in the skin and cracked or broken bones.

Selecting and Storing Meats, Poultry, and Game

Be sure to wrap your meats, poultry, and game in air-permeable paper (butcher's paper). They can be stored in the refrigerator at 38 degrees F for a couple of days. However, if these meats are fresh, they have a short shelf life, so if they will not be cooked and consumed within 2 to 3 days, freezing them is recommended.

Always keep and store meats, poultry, and game separately to prevent cross-contamination.

Country-Style Barbecue Ribs

Making these ribs on top of the stove is an alternate way to prepare wonderful country-style barbecue. It's important to make sure
that there's enough liquid in the skillet while they're cooking.

3 pounds pork spare ribs, cut   2 cups Barbecue Sauce, see
   into serving pieces   recipe on page 127
2 tablespoons seasoning salt

Wash and pat dry the spare rib pieces; sprinkle with seasoning
salt and set aside. Pour 2 cups water into a large, heavy-bottomed
skillet or Dutch oven and bring to a boil over high heat. Place the
seasoned ribs in the boiling water, cover the skillet with a lid,
reduce the heat to medium, and let simmer for about 1 hour.
Remove the ribs and pour out the remaining water. Then, pour
the Barbecue Sauce into the skillet and bring to boil over medium
heat. Add the ribs and reduce the heat to low, cover, and cook
about 30 minutes or until the ribs are tender.

Makes 6 to 8 servings.

Duck with Turnips

Boneless, skinless chicken breasts can be used in this recipe
instead of duck, or portabella mushrooms can be substituted for
the duck to make a vegetarian version. I enjoy serving duck with
turnips over freshly baked buttermilk cornbread.

2 tablespoons olive oil

1 pound turnips, peeled, cut
    into 1-inch cubes

1 cup chopped celery

1 cup chopped carrots

1 pound boneless, skinless
    duck breast, cut into
    1-inch cubes

1 teaspoon salt

½ teaspoon white pepper

½ cup dry white wine

Heat the olive oil in a large sauté pan over medium heat for 1 minute or until hot, but not smoky. Add the turnips, celery, and carrots and sauté for about 5 minutes or until the vegetables turn semi-soft. Stir in the duck breast, salt, pepper, and wine. Cover the sauté pan with a lid, reduce the heat to low, and simmer about 20 minutes, stirring occasionally.

Makes 4 to 6 servings.

Eggplant with Chicken Tenders

Zucchini can be substituted for the eggplant in this recipe, and saltine crackers can be used instead of seasoned bread crumbs for the topping.

¼ cup vegetable oil

1 large eggplant (about 1
    pound), peeled, cut into
    1-inch cubes

1 cup diced onions

1 cup diced sweet red bell
    peppers

2 pounds chicken tenders, cut
    into 1-inch pieces

½ cup freshly chopped
    parsley

2 tablespoons Worcestershire
    sauce

2 cups seasoned bread crumbs

Heat the vegetable oil in a large skillet over medium heat for 2 minutes or until hot. Add the eggplant cubes, onions, and red bell pepper and sauté for 5 minutes or until soft. Stir in the chicken pieces, parsley, and Worcestershire sauce, cover the skillet with a lid, and let simmer about 5 minutes, stirring occasionally. Remove the lid and sprinkle the seasoned bread crumbs on top. Place the skillet under the broiler for about 1 minute or until the bread crumbs are brown and toasted.

Makes 6 to 8 servings.

Ham and Mixed Greens

I like serving this dish sandwiched inside freshly baked homemade rolls or biscuits as an appetizer at luncheons or dinners. Note: Once the ham and greens are cooked, they must be drained well before they are spread on baked rolls or biscuits.

1 pound fresh arugula	**2 tablespoons red wine**
1 pound fresh spinach	**(optional)**
2 tablespoons butter	
1 pound smoke-cured ham,	
cut into ½-inch cubes	

Wash the arugula and spinach, pat dry with paper towels, and chop coarsely. Melt the butter in a medium-size saucepan over medium heat. Add the ham cubes and sauté until they turn slightly brown. Stir in the wine, arugula, and spinach, cover the saucepan with a lid, and cook about 10 minutes, stirring occasionally. Remove the lid and continue to cook until all the juices have evaporated.

Makes 4 to 6 servings.

Hot and Spicy Chicken

My grandfather, Frank Randle, loved hot and spicy foods. He once told me that he got his taste buds from his father, Joe Randle. Grandfather made some of the best spicy spaghetti. I can still remember more than thirty years ago, when the tears used to roll down my face while I ate it, but at the same time I would be smiling because the flavor of his spaghetti was so tasty, even beyond the hot peppers. This is one of my favorite recipes. I think about my grandfather whenever I make it.

2 pounds chicken thighs
1 tablespoon seasoned salt
1 teaspoon garlic powder
½ cup vegetable oil
2 cups chopped onions
3 cups tomatoes, freshly
   chopped
1 cup of chicken broth
1 teaspoon sugar
3 jalapeño peppers, freshly
   chopped

Wash and pat dry the chicken thighs with paper towels, then sprinkle with seasoned salt and garlic powder and set them aside. Heat the vegetable oil in a large skillet or Dutch oven over medium heat until hot. Add the chicken thighs and fry about 5 minutes on each side or until browned, then set aside. Pour out all but 2 tablespoons of the oil, add the onions, and sauté about 3 minutes or until soft. Stir in the tomatoes, chicken broth, sugar, and jalapeño peppers, cover the skillet with a lid, and let simmer about 20 minutes, stirring occasionally. Add the chicken thighs back to the skillet, cover the skillet again. Reduce the heat to low, and cook about 1 hour.

Makes 6 to 8 servings.

Kidney and Mushrooms

I prefer using calf or veal kidney for this recipe because it gives a richer taste. Like most organs, calf or veal kidney requires preparation before it can be cooked. The first step is to pull away all the fat that surrounds the kidney, then peel off the covering membrane and discard it. Cut the ducts from the center (without damaging the kidney), then cut the kidney into cubes before cooking it. This stage is necessary and involves double-checking for ducts that could be hidden within the flesh of the kidney.

1 pound calf or veal kidney
3 tablespoons butter
½ cup of beef or vegetable
    broth
1 pound chopped white
    button mushrooms
½ tablespoon chopped garlic
½ teaspoon black pepper

Prepare the kidney according to the steps described in the headnote above. Heat the butter in a medium-size frying pan over medium heat until melted. Add the kidney cubes and sauté about 5 minutes or until they turn slightly brown. Pour in the beef broth, add the mushrooms, garlic, and pepper; cover the skillet with a lid and let simmer about 15 minutes. Add more butter if necessary.

Makes 4 to 6 servings.

Smoked Sausage with Carrots and Raisins

I came up with this recipe about ten years ago. It was inspired by my friend Katherine Kraff, who used to make her version with sauerkraut and onions, served on firm hot dog buns.

1 pound good quality smoked sausages

3 large banana peppers, such as banana chili, yellow-green peppers with a mild flavor

3 cups shredded carrots

1 cup beef broth

½ cup raisins

¼ cup dried dark currants

Place the smoked sausages in a large skillet and cook them over medium heat until they turn slightly brown. Add the remaining ingredients plus 1 cup of water, cover the skillet with a lid, and let cook for 15 minutes. Remove the lid and continue to cook until all the liquid has absorbed, stirring frequently.

Makes 6 to 8 servings.

Supper Stew

This is a quick and easy way to make a pot of gumbo. It's important to use the freshest ingredients available to make this supper stew taste great. I like serving it over toasted French or Italian bread, cooked white rice, or pasta.

4 cups chopped fresh
    tomatoes
1 bay leaf
1 cup chicken or vegetable
    broth
1 teaspoon sugar
3 dashes Tabasco sauce
1 pound boneless, skinless
    chicken breasts, cut into
    1-inch pieces

1 pound fresh medium-size
    shrimp, shell on
½ pound smoked sausage,
    sliced into ½-inch pieces
1 dozen oysters, cleaned

Place the tomatoes, bay leaf, chicken broth, sugar, and Tabasco sauce in a large, heavy-bottomed skillet or Dutch oven. Bring to a boil over high heat, then reduce to medium, cover the skillet, and let simmer for 20 minutes. Add the chicken, shrimp, and smoked sausage; cover and cook about 20 minutes. Add the oysters and cook uncovered about 10 minutes. Remove the bay leaf and serve.

Makes 6 to 8 servings.

Sweetbreads

Sweetbreads are the thymus and pancreatic glands of young animals such as calves or lambs. These glands tend to shrink and become tough as the animals get older and their diet changes from milk to grain. Sweetbreads must be soaked in cold water for about two hours before using. Afterward, they must be cleaned by cutting away any discolored parts, then they must be blanched for about 5 minutes. The glands can then be braised or poached in milk or a broth, sautéed in butter, or deep fried.

1 pound sweetbreads	1 teaspoon all-purpose flour
3 tablespoons butter	2 cups half & half
¼ cup finely chopped onions	salt and black pepper to taste

Soak the sweetbreads in cold water for about 2 hours, then drain them and set aside. Place 2 cups water in a large skillet and bring to boil over high heat. Add the sweetbreads and boil for about 5 minutes, then let cool. Remove the outer membrane, and cut the sweetbreads into small pieces. Pour the water out of the skillet, place the butter in it, and melt over medium heat. Add the sweetbreads and onions and sauté until they turn slightly brown. Sprinkle in the flour, half & half, salt, and pepper. Reduce the heat to low, cover the skillet, and simmer about 10 minutes. Serve with cooked string beans or toast.

Makes 4 to 6 servings.

Veal Chops

Veal comes from calves age 3 to 6 months. It tastes best when the animal is fed on milk instead of grain, because the meat is more tender and pink. My mother rarely cooked veal, but occasionally she would make smothered veal chops (also called veal cutlets), served with egg noodles.

2 pounds veal chops, ½-inch
    thick
3 teaspoons mustard
1 teaspoon salt
¼ teaspoon ground nutmeg
½ cup all-purpose flour
2 tablespoons vegetable oil

1½ cups finely chopped
    onions
1½ cups chicken broth
½ cup fresh dill, finely
    chopped
½ cup sour cream

Pound the veal chops with a mallet until they are about ¼-inch thick. Spread mustard on both sides, then sprinkle with salt and nutmeg. Pour the flour on a large plate and dredge the seasoned chops until both sides are well coated. Heat the vegetable oil in a large, heavy-bottomed skillet over medium heat until hot. Fry each veal chop about 3 or 4 minutes on each side, then remove to a plate. Sauté the onions in the remaining oil about 2 minutes or until soft. Add the chicken broth and chops, cover, reduce the heat to low, and let simmer 30 minutes or until the chops are tender. Stir in the dill and sour cream and cook, uncovered, 5 minutes longer, stirring occasionally. Serve with egg noodles or rice.

Makes 4 to 6 servings.

Beef Burgundy

On February 12, 2005, I hosted a wonderful celebration in tribute to my good friend Julia Child (also known as The French Chef). It was held at Kendall College in Chicago. With the help of Kendall's wonderful staff and culinary arts students, we put together a menu of Julia's favorite foods, including her famous boeuf bourguignon (beef stew in red wine with onions and mushrooms). She had many Americans running to their kitchens to make this dish during the early 1960s.

This recipe is similar to Julia's version, but I call it beef burgundy because a whole bottle of burgundy wine is used.

¼ cup olive oil
2 pounds boneless beef stew
    meat, cut into 1-inch
    pieces
2 cups coarsely chopped
    onions
2 cups coarsely chopped
    white button mushrooms

5 cups (about 1 bottle) red
    wine (burgundy
    preferred)
1½ cups Burgundy Sauce, see
    recipe on page 128
1 teaspoon cornstarch
    (optional)
salt and black pepper to taste

Pour the oil in a heavy-bottomed saucepan or Dutch oven and heat over high until the oil starts simmering (without smoking). Add the beef and brown on all sides, about 2 minutes each side. Transfer the browned meat to a large bowl and set aside. Sauté the onions and mushrooms in the remaining oil in the saucepan until soft. Add the meat back to the saucepan, pour in the wine and Burgundy Sauce, reduce the heat to low, cover the saucepan, and let simmer about 2 hours or until the beef is very tender. For a thicker sauce, stir in 1 teaspoon of cornstarch once the beef is done. Season the beef burgundy with salt and pepper and serve hot.

Makes 6 to 8 servings.

Calf's Liver with Onions and Gravy

I have bad memories about eating liver when I was young. I didn't like it because my family overcooked it. They would coat it with flour, salt, and pepper, then fry it and smother it in gravy. It tasted very bitter, and had a grainy, shoe-leather texture. One of my good friends later taught me how to cook liver, and I was told: *Don't cook the hell out of it!*

1 pound fresh calf's liver, cut
    into quarters
½ cup all purpose flour
1 teaspoon salt
½ teaspoon black pepper

3 tablespoons vegetable oil
1½ cups Brown Sauce
    (gravy), see recipe on
    page 128

Wash the liver quarters under cold water, pat them dry, and set aside. Mix together the flour, salt, and black pepper in a re-sealable plastic bag. Place each piece of liver in the plastic bag, and shake to coat with the seasoned flour. Meanwhile, heat the oil in a large sauté pan or frying pan over low heat about 2 minutes or until hot. Add the liver pieces, cover the sauté pan, and brown slowly, about 10 to 12 minutes on each side. Pour in the Brown Sauce, cover again, and let simmer about 3 to 5 minutes. Serve with mashed potatoes.

Makes 2 to 4 servings.

Chicken Breasts with Sage Barbecue Sauce

The chicken breasts used in this recipe can be cut into 2-inch strips once they are cooked and served on top of fries. Chicken breast strips can also be served on top of Italian bread with lettuce, tomatoes, and bean sprouts.

2 pounds boneless, skinless
    chicken breast halves
1 tablespoon fresh oregano (or
    1 teaspoon dried)
1 tablespoon fresh rosemary
    (or 1 teaspoon dried)
½ cup all purpose flour

¼ cup vegetable oil
2 cups Barbecue Sauce, see
    recipe on page 127
1 tablespoon chopped fresh
    sage (or 1 teaspoon
    dried)

Wash the chicken breast halves and pat dry with paper towels. Season them with oregano and rosemary, then dredge each piece through the flour to coat completely. Set aside. Heat the oil in a large skillet or sauce pan over high heat about 1 minute until hot. Fry each piece of chicken for about 5 minutes on each side or until golden brown, and set them on a plate. Pour the reserve oil out of the skillet and wipe the skillet clean with a paper towel. Pour the Barbecue Sauce in the skillet, add the sage, and cook over medium heat until it starts to boil. Add the chicken breasts, cover the skillet, and let simmer for about 20 minutes or until the chicken is tender.

Makes 4 to 6 servings.

Chicken Creole

I met the late chef Austin Leslie, former chef and owner of Chez Helene's, New Orleans, about fifteen years ago at his restaurant. Many of us food-loving folks thought the 1980s CBS comedy show "Frank's Place" was just like Chef Helene's restaurant—a meeting place where all types of folks, wealthy and poor, would meet and break bread together.

Chef Austin made me some of the best New Orleans–style cooking that I ever tasted. I asked him about several of his Creole dishes, all containing onions, sweet green bell peppers, and celery. He told me that this "trinity" of ingredients is used in most Cajun and Creole dishes.

A whole chicken, cut up into serving pieces, can be used in this recipe instead of thighs. I like using dark meat because it lends more flavor.

½ cup vegetable oil
½ cup all purpose flour
2 cups diced onions
1 cup diced sweet green bell peppers
1 cup diced celery

2 tablespoons tomato paste
5 cups diced tomatoes
1 teaspoon sugar
2 pounds chicken thighs
1 bay leaf

To make the roux: Pour the oil into a large, heavy-bottomed skillet or a Dutch oven and heat over a low flame for about 2 minutes or until the oil starts to simmer. Sprinkle in the flour and stir constantly with a wooden spoon or a whisk for about 10 minutes to reach a peanut butter brown–color roux.

Turn the heat up to high, add the onions, green peppers, and celery to the roux, and sauté for about 4 minutes or until soft. Add the remaining ingredients, reduce the heat to low, cover the skillet, and let cook about 2½ hours, stirring about every 15 minutes.

Makes 6 to 8 servings.

Chicken and Dumplings

Fresh herbs such as oregano, chives, and parsley can be added to the dumplings before cooking them.

1 cup all purpose flour
¼ teaspoon salt
1¼ teaspoons baking powder
¼ teaspoon cayenne pepper
⅓ cup whole milk
2 pounds boneless, skinless
    chicken breasts, cut into
    1½-inch cubes

4 cups chicken broth
1 cup chopped celery
1 cup chopped carrots, peeled
¼ cup freshly chopped
    parsley

To make the dumplings: Combine the flour, salt, baking powder, and cayenne pepper together in a medium-size mixing bowl. Add the milk and mix well, cover the bowl with plastic wrap, and set aside.

Place the chicken, broth, celery, carrots, and three cups of water (to balance the flavor and dilute the salt from the broth) in a large pot or Dutch oven. Bring to a boil over high heat, then reduce to medium, cover the pot, and let simmer about 1½ hours. Drop teaspoons of the dumpling mixture into the simmering pot, cover, and cook about 20 minutes. Sprinkle with parsley and serve hot.

Makes 6 to 8 servings.

Smothered Chicken

Sylvia Woods makes some of the best smothered chicken at Sylvia's, her flagship restaurant in Harlem. Whenever I'm in New York, I usually swing by and have a plate of her smothered chicken with mashed potatoes, a side order of collard greens, and a slice of pound cake.

In my smothered chicken recipe, I like adding a few extra ingredients such as fresh mushrooms, green bell peppers, and onions.

1 2½- to 3-pound whole chicken
salt and black pepper to taste
½ cup all purpose flour
½ cup vegetable oil
1 cup coarsely chopped mushrooms
½ cup chopped green bell peppers
½ cup chopped onions
1½ cups chicken broth

Wash the chicken under cool water, pat dry with paper towels, and cut into serving pieces. Sprinkle salt and pepper on each piece and dredge through the flour, coating lightly. Heat the oil in a large, heavy-bottomed skillet over medium heat about 2 minutes or until hot. Fry the chicken pieces about 4 minutes on each side or until browned. Reserve about 2 tablespoons of oil in the skillet and pour out the rest. Sauté the mushrooms, green bell peppers, and onions in the oil for about 3 minutes or until soft. Return the chicken to the skillet, and add the chicken broth. Reduce the heat to low and let simmer for about 45 minutes, turning the chicken every 10 minutes. Add more broth during cooking if needed.

Makes 6 to 8 servings.

Chicken Fried Steak

I remember when I was about nine years old, my next-door neighbor, Ms. Nancy Johnson, made some chicken fried steak. I was so confused by the name, I thought I was eating chicken. Ms. Johnson was a fabulous cook who worked at a restaurant in New York City for many years before returning to the south. She assured me that I would love chicken fried steak, especially her's — and she was right.

1 pound beef steak, about ¾-inch thick, cut into 4 round pieces	½ teaspoon black pepper
	½ teaspoon garlic powder
	¼ cup vegetable oil
½ cup all purpose flour	1½ cups beef broth or water
½ teaspoon salt	½ cup diced onions

Using a meat mallet or rolling pin, pound the steak to about ½-inch thickness. Place the flour, salt, black pepper, and garlic powder on a large piece of wax paper and mix together. Dredge each piece of steak in the flour mixture to coat completely. Heat the vegetable oil in a large frying pan over medium heat until hot. Add the steak pieces and cook about 3 minutes on each side. Add the beef broth and onions, cover the frying pan, and continue to cook about 25 to 30 minutes, turning the meat every 10 minutes. Add more broth if necessary.

Makes 4 servings.

Chicken and Gravy

Chicken thighs or wings can be substituted in this recipe.

1 tablespoon garlic powder
2 teaspoons onion powder
1 teaspoon sweet paprika
½ teaspoon ground black
   pepper
½ teaspoon salt

½ cup all purpose flour
2 pounds chicken drumsticks
½ cup vegetable oil
2½ cups Brown Sauce, see
   recipe on page 128

Combine garlic powder, onion powder, sweet paprika, black pepper, salt, and flour in a re-sealable plastic bag. Wash the chicken and pat dry with paper towels. Place each piece of chicken in the plastic bag, shake well, and set aside. Heat the oil in a large frying pan over medium heat for 2 minutes or until hot. Cook the chicken pieces for about 3 minutes on each side or until browned, then remove from the pan. Pour out the oil and wipe the frying pan clean. Pour the Brown Sauce in the pan and heat over low heat until hot. Put the chicken back in the pan, cover, and cook about 35 to 40 minutes or until tender.

Makes 6 to 8 servings.

Chicken and Rice

This recipe calls for chicken wings. You can also try grilling them instead of frying. The grilled flavor complements the rice.

1 pound chicken wings	1½ cups Herbal Sauce, see
1 teaspoon salt	recipe on page 131
¼ teaspoon ground black	2 cups long-grain white rice
pepper	1 teaspoon salt
2 tablespoons vegetable oil	

Wash the wings, pat dry with paper towels, season with salt and pepper, and set aside. Heat the oil in a large frying pan over medium heat for 2 minutes until hot. Fry the wings in the oil for about 4 minutes on each side or until they are browned. Remove the wings from the pan. Pour out the oil and wipe the frying pan clean. Pour in the Herbal Sauce and heat over medium heat until it starts to boil. Add the wings, cover, and let simmer about 40 minutes or until they are tender.

Bring 4 cups of water to boil. Stir in the rice and 1 teaspoon salt, reduce the heat to low, cover, and simmer about 20 minutes or until the rice grains are soft and the liquid has absorbed. Serve the chicken over the rice.

Makes 4 to 6 servings.

Chicken Livers and Rice

When I was in my early thirties, I attended the Ecole de Gastronomique Francaise Ritz-Escoffier in Paris. This is a small cooking school located in the world-famous Ritz Hotel. Although I ate many, many meals at the hotel's signature restaurant, Espandon, I also enjoyed having simple but delicious-tasting foods in some of Paris's cafes, bistros, and brasseries. One of my all-time favorites was the Salade de Foies de Volailles Tiedes (Salad of Warm Sautéed Chicken Livers) at the Le Grand Corona restaurant, located in the chic part of Paris where many fashion clothing designers have stores. This delicious dish was made of chicken livers sautéed in butter, port wine, crème fraiche, salt, and pepper, served over red leaf lettuce with a splash of sherry vinegar and a sprinkle of fresh chervil.

In my version of chicken livers, I smother them with corn and serve over rice, which adds a down-home southern touch.

1 pound fresh chicken livers	1 cup fresh corn kernels
½ teaspoon salt	¼ cup port wine
½ teaspoon black pepper	2 tablespoons cider vinegar
2 tablespoons vegetable oil	1 cup white long grain rice
2 tablespoons butter	½ teaspoon salt
¼ cup chopped shallots	

Trim the chicken livers of any membrane and cut into pieces. Season the pieces with salt and pepper. Heat the oil and butter in a medium-size sauté pan over medium heat for 1 minute until hot (but not smoky). Sauté the shallots for 1 minute, then add the livers, corn, port wine, and cider vinegar, reduce the heat to low, and sauté for 2 minutes. Cover the skillet and let simmer about 2 to 3 minutes. Remove the sauté pan from heat and set aside.

Bring 2 cups of water to a boil in a medium-size pot. Stir in the rice and salt. Reduce the heat to low, cover the pot, and cook for about 20 minutes or until the rice is soft and the water is absorbed. Spoon the cooked rice onto a serving platter and top with the smothered livers.

Makes 4 servings.

Chili with Beef Cubes

Cubes of chicken breast can be substituted for the beef cubes in this recipe. For a vegetarian version, canned kidney beans can be used.

2 tablespoons vegetable oil
2 pounds beef (preferably chuck, trimmed of excess fat), cut into 1½-inch cubes
2 cups diced onions
1 cup diced sweet green bell peppers
1 tablespoon chopped fresh garlic

4 cups diced tomatoes
2 tablespoons chili powder
1 teaspoon salt
1 tablespoon sugar
2 tablespoons Worcestershire sauce
2 cups Tomato Sauce, see recipe on page 133
3 to 4 dashes Tabasco sauce

Heat the vegetable oil in a large pot or Dutch oven over high heat for 2 minutes or until hot. Add the beef and brown it on all sides. Add the remaining ingredients plus 2 cups water. Cover, reduce the heat to medium, and let simmer about 2 hours or until the meat is tender.

Makes 8 servings.

Creole Duck

My family didn't eat a lot of duck: we had it annually, during the holiday season. I love duck and I loved my mother's duck dressing. She would first roast the duck, then use the reserved juices, fat, liver, and neck to make what we call a "rich" dressing.

I use duck breasts in this Creole recipe. Six cups of the Creole Sauce on page 130 can be substituted for the sauce ingredients listed below (onions, green bell peppers, yellow peppers, celery, tomatoes, and chicken broth). A whole duck, cut into serving pieces, can also be used instead of the duck breasts.

⅓ cup vegetable oil

2 cups diced onions

1½ cups chopped sweet green bell peppers

1½ cups chopped sweet yellow bell peppers

1½ cups chopped celery

6 cups diced tomatoes

2 cups chicken broth

1 tablespoon sugar

1 teaspoon dried thyme

½ teaspoon rosemary

4 duck breasts, cut in halves with skin attached (or a 2-pound whole duck, cut into serving pieces)

Heat the vegetable oil in a large pot or Dutch oven over medium heat for 2 minutes or until hot. Cook the onions, bell peppers, and celery until soft. Add the tomatoes, broth, sugar, thyme, and rosemary. Cover the pot and cook about 15 minutes. Add the duck breasts, cover the pot again, and cook about 90 minutes or until the duck breasts are tender.

Makes 6 servings.

Ham and Apples

This recipe also works very well with leftover roasted turkey, along with some sweet potatoes, cranberries, and chopped walnuts.

1½ cups honey
½ cup unsalted butter
1 pound ham, cut into 2-inch cubes
¼ teaspoon ground cinnamon
⅛ teaspoon ground allspice
½ cup raisins
2 cups peeled, cored, coarsely chopped apples (Granny Smith or firm cooking apple)

½ cup coarsely chopped walnuts
2 cups marshmallows (for topping)
⅛ teaspoon freshly grated nutmeg

Heat the honey and butter in a medium-size skillet over low heat until they are melted together. Add the remainder of the ingredients except the marshmallows and nutmeg, cover the skillet, and let simmer about 15 minutes, stirring occasionally. Remove the lid and cover the top of the ham mixture with marshmallows and sprinkle with nutmeg. Place the skillet under the broiler for 1 minute or until the marshmallows start to brown.

Makes 4 to 6 servings.

Ham and Red-Eye Gravy

My late great-grandmother, Ada, had a smokehouse and she cured her own hams, which tasted wonderful. When my younger sister Denise and I would spend the night at her home, we looked forward to morning because my great-grandmother always made a delicious breakfast of ham and red-eye gravy and homemade biscuits.

Red-eye gravy is a thin gravy made from ham drippings and water—sometimes it's flavored with coffee. Grandmamma Ada never used coffee, but instead would add a little flour, salt, and black pepper to ham drippings. Sometimes she would fry the ham, then cut it up into small pieces and add it to the gravy and serve over piping hot biscuits.

½ teaspoon vegetable oil
4 to 6 thin slices ham (with fat attached)
1 cup hot water or coffee
½ teaspoon salt
¼ teaspoon black pepper
1½ teaspoons all purpose flour

Heat the vegetable oil in a large skillet over medium heat for 2 minutes or until hot. Add the ham and fry about 1 minute on both sides. Remove the ham and pour in the hot water, salt, pepper and flour. Stir constantly using a whisk or fork, scraping up the brown bits, until the liquid turns into a smooth sauce. Return the ham to the skillet, cover, and let simmer about 3 to 5 minutes. Pour the gravy and ham over freshly cooked biscuits or grits.

Makes 4 to 6 servings.

Smothered Lamb Chops

My mother didn't cook lamb when I was growing up, she didn't like the taste. On the other hand, I love lamb and all the wonderful dishes that can be made by using it. I serve some type of lamb at least once a month, so I guess this craving can be called catching up from my childhood.

This is one of my signature dishes, and it tastes even better the next day, once the flavors have had time to come together.

4 4-ounce lamb chops
salt and black pepper to taste
3 tablespoons vegetable oil
2 cups peeled, diced sweet
    potatoes

2 cups Brown Sauce, see
    recipe on page 128

Wash the lamb chops under cool water and pat dry with paper towels. Season the chops with salt and black pepper and set aside. Heat 2 tablespoons of vegetable oil in a large frying pan over medium heat for 2 minutes or until hot. Cook the chops about 4 minutes on each side or until they turn brown, and set them aside. Add 1 tablespoon of vegetable oil to the skillet and sauté the sweet potatoes about 10 minutes or until they turn soft.

Pour 2 cups of Brown Sauce over the potatoes, return the chops back to the skillet, cover with a lid, reduce the heat to low, and let simmer about 25 minutes, turning the chops and stirring the potatoes every 3 to 4 minutes.

Makes 4 servings.

Lamb Shanks

Lamb chops can be quite expensive at the butcher's or grocery store. However, lamb shanks (the lower portion of the leg) are always reasonably priced and are great for grilling and smothering.

2 8-ounce lamb shanks
salt and black pepper to taste
2 tablespoons olive oil
1 large sweet green bell
    pepper, seeded and thinly
    sliced
1 large sweet red bell pepper,
    seeded and thinly sliced

1 large white onion, peeled
    and thinly sliced
3 cups Mushroom Sauce, see
    recipe on page 132
½ cup dry white wine
1 bay leaf

Wash the lamb shanks under cool water and pat dry with paper towels. Season with salt and pepper and set aside. Heat the olive oil in a large saucepan or Dutch oven over high heat for 1 minute or until hot. Place the seasoned shanks in the pan and brown on all sides. Remove the shanks and set them aside on a plate. Put the bell peppers and onion in the pan and cook over medium heat about 5 minutes or until they turn soft. Return the shanks to the saucepan along with the Mushroom Sauce, wine, and bay leaf. Cover and let simmer about 1½ hours or until the shanks are cooked and tender.

Makes 2 to 4 servings.

Grown-up Sloppy Joes

When I was a kid, I loved Sloppy Joes. My family bought the Hunts Manwich commercial brand sauce and doctored it up with fresh chopped onions, green bell peppers, barbecue sauce, American cheese, and plenty of ground beef, and served it on hamburger buns. Because Mother considered this to be junk food (a term used before "fast food" was vogue), we couldn't have Sloppy Joes often—every other Friday evening or Saturday afternoon at most.

Here's a grown-up version of Sloppy Joes, containing ground sirloin, mushrooms, Dijon mustard, and Tabasco sauce, among other ingredients.

2 pounds lean ground sirloin
1½ cups diced onions
2 cups ketchup
½ cup brown sugar
1 cup chopped white button
   mushrooms
2 cups Tomato Sauce, see
   recipe on page 133

½ cup Barbecue Sauce, see
   recipe on page 127
2 tablespoons Dijon mustard
   (optional)
3 dashes Tabasco sauce

Heat a large nonstick skillet over medium heat about 1 minute. Add the ground sirloin and cook until it turns brown, stirring frequently. Add onions and continue to cook for 5 minutes. Add the remaining ingredients, stir thoroughly, cover the skillet, and cook about 30 minutes. Serve over Kaiser rolls or cooked pasta.

Makes 6 to 8 servings.

Orange Duck Breasts

Raspberry- or lavender and honey–flavored duck breasts can be used instead of orange in this recipe. For raspberry flavor, use fresh or frozen raspberries and raspberry liqueur. For lavender and honey–flavored breasts, use crushed dried lavender flowers along with some honey.

2 6-ounce duck breasts, cut into halves	2 tablespoons orange zest
salt and black pepper to taste	1 teaspoon sugar
1 tablespoon olive oil	½ teaspoon rosemary
2 cups orange juice	½ teaspoon cornstarch

Wash the duck breasts and pat dry. Season with salt and black pepper, then score the skin with a sharp knife (make large lines through the fat). Set aside. Heat the oil in a large sauté pan over medium heat for 1 minute or until hot but not smoky. Place the breasts skin side down in the pan and cook for about 3 minutes. Turn over and cook about 3 more minutes. Remove the breasts from the sauté pan and set aside. Add orange juice, orange zest, sugar, and rosemary and cook about 2 minutes. Put the breasts back in the sauté pan, cover, and reduce heat to low. Simmer about 20 minutes or until the breasts are tender.

Remove the breasts from the sauté pan and let them rest for about 5 minutes before cutting. Turn the heat up to high under the sauté pan and let the reserve sauce cook for about 5 minutes. Stir in the cornstarch and continue to stir until the sauce thickens.

Cut the breasts against the grain of the meat into ½-inch pieces and pour the sauce on top. Serve with steamed vegetables such as broccoli or asparagus.

Makes 2 to 4 servings.

Pepper Steak

To make this recipe using chicken, I replace the steak with chicken breasts cut into 2-inch strips.

2 tablespoons soy sauce
⅓ cup vegetable oil, plus 1
    tablespoon
1 tablespoon chopped garlic
1½ to 2 pounds round steak,
    cut into 2-inch strips
1½ cups Tomato Sauce, see
    recipe on page 133

1 cup coarsely chopped
    onions
2 cups coarsely chopped
    sweet green bell peppers
1 cup coarsely chopped
    tomatoes
1 teaspoon cornstarch
¼ cup water

Combine the soy sauce, vegetable oil, and chopped garlic in a cup and mix well with a fork; set aside. Heat 1 tablespoon vegetable oil in a large saucepan or skillet for 1 minute or until hot. Add the strips of steak and cook until they turn light brown on all sides. Add the soy sauce mixture and the remaining ingredients except the cornstarch and water, reduce the heat to low, and cook about 40 minutes or until the vegetables are soft and the meat is tender. Remove skillet from heat. Mix the cornstarch and water in a small cup and pour over the vegetables and steak in the saucepan; stir until sauce thickens.

Makes 4 to 6 servings.

Pheasant and Cabbage

If you can't find pheasant at the market, substitute quail or duck. Just make sure that the weight is the same as the pheasant used in this recipe.

2 pounds pheasant (about 2 whole birds) cut into serving pieces	2 cups chopped carrots
salt and black pepper to taste	1 cup chopped celery
2 tablespoons olive oil	2½ cups Mushroom Sauce, see recipe on page 132
1 tablespoon butter	1 pound shredded cabbage

Wash the pheasant under cool water and pat dry with paper towels. Season with salt and black pepper and set aside. Heat the olive oil and butter in a medium-size saucepan or Dutch oven over medium heat for 1 minute or until hot. Cook the pheasant until brown on all sides, then remove and set aside. Place the carrots and celery in the saucepan and cook about 4 to 5 minutes until they turn soft. Return the pheasant to the pan, along with Mushroom Sauce and cabbage. Cover the saucepan and simmer about 1 hour over medium heat until the cabbage and pheasant are tender.

Makes 6 to 8 servings.

Smothered Pork Chops

My good friend Edna Stewart makes some of the best smothered pork chops I've ever tasted. For over forty years, Edna's restaurant, called Edna's, has been located on the west side of Chicago. She loves to share her stories with friends and customers at the restaurant. One of my favorites is about how she fed many of the freedom riders during the civil rights movement of the 1960s, often for free because many of them didn't have money to pay. But for Edna, serving a good cause was payment enough.

Freshly chopped mushrooms (about 2 cups) can be added to this recipe, after the gravy has been made.

4 ¾-inch-thick pork chops	½ cup vegetable oil
salt and black pepper to taste	2 cups coarsely chopped
1 cup all purpose flour, plus 2	onions
tablespoons	1¼ cups water

Wash the pork chops under cool water and pat dry with paper towels. Season the chops with salt and black pepper and set aside. Pour 1 cup of flour on chopping board or flat surface. Dredge the chops through the flour so they are well coated. Heat the vegetable oil in a large heavy-bottomed skillet over medium heat for 2 minutes or until hot. Fry the chops about 5 minutes on each side until they are well browned. Place them on a plate and set aside. Pour off all but 2 tablespoons of oil and drippings from the skillet. Sauté the onions over medium heat for about 5 minutes or until they are soft. Set the sautéed onions on top of the pork chops on the plate. Add 2 tablespoons of flour to the drippings in the skillet. Gradually pour 1 cup of water in the skillet and stir until the mixture becomes a smooth gravy. Add salt and black pepper to taste. Put the onions and pork chops on top of the gravy, cover, reduce heat, and simmer about 15 minutes or until the chops are tender. Add more water if necessary.

Makes 4 servings.

Smothered Rabbit

WILBERT JONES

A visit at my late friend Julia Child's apartment in Santa Barbara, CA, along with Ramona Douglass, October 4, 2003.

On October 4, 2003, I made this recipe for my friend Julia Child. She told me that she was craving for some smothered rabbit, but was having difficulty locating rabbit in Santa Barbara, California, where she was living at the time. I brought two rabbits out to her apartment and made us a nice old-fashioned lunch of smothered rabbit, herb roasted potatoes, mixed green salad, and fresh fruit cobbler. We sat on her patio and ate the entire afternoon, while gossiping about everything from the latest and craziest diet trends to the newest must-try food products in the grocery stores.

(1) 2-pound whole rabbit	½ teaspoon dried thyme
1 teaspoon salt	1 teaspoon minced garlic
½ teaspoon white pepper	2 cups chicken broth
1 cup all purpose flour	½ cup dry white wine
½ cup vegetable oil	1 tablespoon all purpose flour
1 cup diced onions	1 tablespoon chopped parsley,
½ cup diced celery	for garnish
½ cup diced carrots	

Wash the rabbit in cold water and pat dry with paper towels. Cut the rabbit into 6 or 8 serving pieces and season with salt and white pepper. Place the flour into a re-sealable plastic bag, drop each piece of rabbit into the bag, and shake to coat with flour. Heat the vegetable oil in a large, heavy-bottomed skillet over medium heat for 2 minutes or until hot. Fry the rabbit pieces for about 5 minutes on both sides or until brown. Set the browned rabbit pieces aside. Add the onions, celery, and carrots to the skillet with the reserve oil and drippings and sauté about 5 minutes or until soft. Stir in the thyme and garlic, cook 3 minutes longer. Put the rabbit pieces back in the skillet along with the chicken broth and wine, reduce the heat to medium low, cover the skillet, and cook about 1½ hours or until the rabbit is very tender, turning the rabbit every 10 to 15 minutes. Add more broth if necessary. After 1½ hours of cooking, stir in 1 tablespoon flour to thicken the sauce. Garnish with chopped parsley and serve over roasted potatoes.

Makes 6 servings.

Steak and Potatoes

I recommend using a nice marble cut of beef containing thin lines of fat for this recipe, such as a New York strip or porterhouse. For more flavor, marinate the meat ahead of time with your favorite rub. I like serving both the steak and potatoes on a Kaiser roll or warm French bread.

½ teaspoon garlic powder
½ teaspoon onion powder
½ teaspoon salt
¼ teaspoon cayenne pepper
¼ teaspoon celery salt
1 teaspoon sweet paprika
¼ teaspoon black pepper
⅛ teaspoon curry powder

2 8-ounce steaks
2 tablespoons vegetable oil
2 cups Burgundy Sauce, see
    recipe on page 128
2 large Idaho potatoes,
    washed, peeled, soaked in
    cold water
2 cups peanut oil, for frying

Combine all the spices and seasonings together in a small bowl and mix well. Wash the steak under cool water and pat dry with paper towels. Rub equal amounts of the seasoning mixture on both sides of the steaks. Heat the vegetable oil in a large skillet over medium heat for 1 minute or until hot. Put the steaks in the skillet and brown about 3 minutes on each side, then pour in the Burgundy Sauce. Reduce heat to low, cover the skillet, and let simmer about 20 minutes.

Meanwhile, take the potatoes out of the water and cut them into ½-inch wedges. Heat the peanut oil in a medium-size pot to

325 degrees F. Fry the potatoes about 2 to 3 minutes or until they turn golden brown and float at the top of the oil. Place them on paper towels and sprinkle lightly with salt.

Once the steaks have been simmering for 20 minutes, remove from the skillet and cut into 3-inch strips. Serve the strips of steak with the Burgundy Sauce over the cooked potatoes.

Makes 2 to 4 servings.

Swiss Steak

This Swiss steak recipe can be made with chuck steak or other less expensive cut of beef.

3 pounds chuck steak, cut
    into 1½-inch cubes
salt and black pepper to taste
1 cup all purpose flour
⅓ cup vegetable oil
2 cups coarsely chopped
    tomatoes

2 cups coarsely chopped
    onions
1 cup peeled, coarsely
    chopped carrots
1 cup coarsely chopped celery
2 cups beef broth

Season the steak cubes with salt and black pepper. Pour the flour in a re-sealable plastic bag. Put a few pieces of steak cubes in the bag of flour at a time and shake to coat. Heat the vegetable oil in a large saucepan or Dutch oven over medium heat for 2 minutes or until hot. Brown the steak cubes on all sides, then add the remaining ingredients. Reduce the heat to medium low, cover the saucepan, and let simmer about 1½ hours or until the vegetables are soft and the beef cubes are tender.

Makes 6 to 8 servings.

Skillet Supper

This recipe reminds me of the freezer clean-out meals my family would make when I was young. It was an excellent way to get rid of food that had been frozen for a while without throwing it out.

1 pound fresh or frozen
    Italian or Polish sausage
½ cup butter or margarine
1 cup chopped onions
½ pound fresh or frozen
    string beans (about 2
    inches long)

2 cups fresh or frozen
    chopped broccoli
2 cups fresh or frozen corn
salt and black pepper to taste
2 cups Herbal Sauce, see
    recipe on page 131

Cut the sausages into 1-inch pieces and set aside. Melt the butter in a large skillet over medium heat. Add the onions to the skillet and sauté until they are soft. Add the sausage pieces and cook about 3 minutes or until they turn brown, stirring constantly. Stir in the remaining ingredients, cover, and let simmer about 20 to 25 minutes or until the vegetables are tender.

Makes 6 to 8 servings.

4

Desserts

About Desserts

I'VE ALWAYS BEEN very passionate about desserts, especially southern desserts. In 1998, this led me to write my second cookbook, *Mama's Tea Cakes: 101 Delicious Soul Food Desserts*, a collection of down-home southern recipes like Fresh Coconut Cake, Moonshine Cake, Tea Cakes, Buttermilk Pie, Sweet Potato Roll, and Fried Apples.

I had the same passion when I started working on the dessert recipes in this book, creating a collection of smothered dessert recipes with real southern down-home taste.

Bananas with Pecans and Whiskey

It has been many years since I had my first Bananas Foster dessert at the famous Brennan's Restaurant in New Orleans. This is where the Bananas Foster was created, using rum that is flambéed so that the strong alcohol flavor is cooked off. I like the alcohol flavor in my dessert, if it calls for alcohol. So this recipe calls for smothering, which is my very own version of Bananas Foster. Brennan's restaurant was also affected by the 2005 Hurricane Katrina disaster.

⅓ cup light brown sugar
½ teaspoon ground cinnamon
¼ teaspoon ground nutmeg
⅓ cup unsalted butter
⅓ cup whiskey

¼ cup chopped pecans
2 tablespoons golden raisins
2 tablespoons dark raisins
4 large bananas, peeled and
    sliced in half, lengthwise

In a small bowl, mix the brown sugar, cinnamon, and nutmeg, and set aside. Melt the butter in a medium-size heavy frying pan over medium heat. Add the sugar mixture and cook until it turns syrupy. Reduce the heat and slowly add the whiskey, constantly stirring for about 1 minute. Add the pecans, raisins, and sliced banana halves to the frying pan. Cover and cook about 3 minutes. Serve on top of toasted cinnamon bread or vanilla ice cream.

Makes 4 servings.

Banana Whip

My great-grandmother, Ada Penn, was a wonderful cook. Even though she was my great-grandmother, all of her grandchildren and great-grandchildren called her Grandmamma Ada.

Grandmamma Ada let me make some sugar cookies in her kitchen. I was twelve years old and didn't know much about organization. The cookies turned out great, but I made a big mess. It took me hours to get her kitchen back in order. I learned a valuable lesson that I practice even today: *Clean as you cook!* I remember Grandmamma Ada saying, "These are some really good cookies, but my kitchen looks like a tornado! You got to clean up this mess!"

I told her that the next dessert I make in her kitchen would be a very simple one, using only a few dishes and ingredients. A couple of weeks later, I made this recipe. We both laughed about how simple the recipe was to make compared to the sugar cookie mess I'd made weeks before.

¼ cup butter	½ cup chopped pecans or walnuts
1 tablespoon sugar	
4 large ripe bananas, cut in half lengthwise	1 4-ounce chocolate candy bar, broken into bite-size pieces
¼ teaspoon ground cinnamon	
1 quart vanilla ice cream	

Melt the butter and sugar in a large skillet over medium heat. Add the bananas and sprinkle in the cinnamon. Cover and let simmer about 2 minutes. Pour into a large bowl and let cool to room temperature, about 15 minutes. Cover with plastic wrap and refrigerate about 1 hour or until the mixture is chilled. Place scoops of vanilla ice cream on top of the chilled cooked bananas, fold in the chopped pecans, and stir well with a large wooden spoon. Pour onto a serving platter and sprinkle with the chocolate candy pieces. Serve immediately.

Makes 6 servings.

Mixed Berry Cobbler

Frozen berries can be used instead of fresh—just place them in a colander and run cold water over them to remove the ice.

1¼ cups graham cracker crumbs (about 15 or 16 crackers)

3 cups fresh blueberries

1 cup fresh raspberries

1 cup fresh blackberries

½ cup golden raisins

½ cup dark raisins

1 cup softened butter, plus ¼ cup

1½ cups sugar, plus ¼ cup

½ teaspoon ground cinnamon

¼ teaspoon ground nutmeg

1 tablespoon freshly squeezed lemon juice

2 teaspoons cornstarch

2 cups whipped cream topping

½ teaspoon cocoa powder

For the graham cracker crust: Mix 1¼ cups of graham cracker crumbs with ¼ cup sugar. Use a pastry blender or fork to blend in ¼ cup butter. Take the back of a spoon and press the buttered crumb mixture into an even layer on the bottom and sides of a 9-inch pie pan, taking care to level the edges of the pie shell. Bake the crust at 375 degrees F for about 8 minutes. Let cool.

Place the remaining ingredients except the cornstarch, whipped cream topping, and cocoa powder in a large sauté pan or saucepan, cover, and heat over low heat for about 15 minutes or until the sugar and butter is melted and the fruit turns soft. Pour the cooked fruit mixture into a large bowl and let cool to room temperature, about 20 minutes. Pour out about ½ cup of the fruit juice and mix it with 2 teaspoons of cornstarch, then pour back into the bowl and mix well with a large wooden spoon to thicken the fruit juices. Pour the fruit and juices into the pie crust and refrigerate uncovered for 2 to 3 hours before serving. Spoon the whipped cream topping on each serving and sprinkle cocoa powder on top.

Makes 6 to 8 servings.

Black Cherries with Walnuts

If you can't find fresh seasonal black cherries, you can substitute frozen black cherries once you've run cool water over them and drained them in a colander. I enjoy serving this recipe over thick slices of pound cake or vanilla ice cream.

½ cup unsalted butter
1 cup sugar
3 cups fresh black cherries, washed, stems removed and pitted
1½ cups seedless dark grapes, sliced in halves

½ cup ground anise seeds (optional)
⅛ teaspoon ground allspice
2 tablespoons bourbon
1 cup chopped walnuts

Melt the butter and sugar in a medium-size skillet over medium heat for about 2 minutes. Add the remaining ingredients, cover the skillet, reduce heat to low, and let simmer about 20 minutes, stirring occasionally.

Makes 4 to 6 servings.

Blackberries and Dumplings

Even today, in Mississippi, blackberries grow wild all over the state during the spring and summer months, and are just loaded with delicious sweet juices. If you have a favorite sugar cookie dough recipe, it can be substituted for the dumplings used here. Also, fresh strawberries and rhubarb can be used instead of blackberries.

1 cup all purpose flour	2 cups vegetable oil, for
¾ teaspoon baking powder	frying
3 tablespoons sugar	2½ cups half & half
¼ cup unsalted butter,	¾ cup sugar
softened	4 cups fresh blackberries
⅓ cup buttermilk	½ teaspoon pure vanilla
¼ teaspoon ground cinnamon	flavoring

Place the flour, baking powder, sugar, butter, buttermilk, and cinnamon in a small bowl and mix with your hands until it turns into a soft ball. Using a rolling pin, roll the dough out about ½-inch thick and cut into 1-inch squares. Heat the vegetable oil in a small saucepan or pot to 375 degrees F and deep fry the dough pieces for about 30 seconds or until they turn golden brown and float to the top of the oil. Place the cooked dough on paper towels to drain off the excess oil.

Heat a medium-size saucepan over medium heat about 1 minute. Add the half & half and sugar and cook about 2 minutes, constantly stirring with a large wooden spoon. Add the fried dough, cover, and cook about 3 to 4 minutes. Add the berries, then the vanilla to flavor, cover again, and cook about 5 minutes longer.

Makes 6 servings.

Bourbon Pumpkin

Once this pie is made, I usually refrigerate it and serve it cold with bourbon ice cream or rum flavored ice cream.

1 cup all purpose flour	½ cup sugar
½ teaspoon salt	1 cup chopped pecans
⅓ cup vegetable shortening	1 cup chopped walnuts
3 teaspoons cold water	¼ cup bourbon
1 cup unsalted butter	2 cups heavy cream
½ cup canned pumpkin puree	1 tablespoon cornstarch

Sift the flour and salt together in a medium-size mixing bowl. Add vegetable shortening and mix with a pastry blender or two knives until the flour mixture forms clumps about the size of oatmeal flakes or small peas. Spoon in the water 1 teaspoon at a time, mixing with a fork after each teaspoon is added. Shape the dough into a ball and flatten it on a lightly floured surface. Roll the dough with the rolling pin from the center to the edge, forming a circle about ⅛-inch thick and about 1 inch longer than the overall size of a 9-inch pie pan. Pick the dough up with a large spatula and place it in the pie pan; press firmly. Trim the edge with a sharp knife so that the dough only extends about ½ inch beyond the edge of the pie pan, then fold the extra ½ inch of dough under the edge. Prick the bottom and sides of the dough with a fork, and bake at 425 degrees F for 12 to 15 minutes or until the crust turns light golden brown.

Meanwhile, place the remaining ingredients except the cornstarch in a large saucepan and heat over medium heat, stirring constantly, for about 2 minutes. Cover the saucepan, reduce heat to low, and let simmer about 20 minutes. Remove the saucepan from the heat and stir in the cornstarch. Pour the fruit mixture in a large bowl, cover, and refrigerate for 2 to 3 hours. Then pour the cold fruit mixture into the pie pan. Place in the oven and bake at 375 degrees F for about 20 minutes or until the pie is set.

Makes 8 servings.

Buttery Cinnamon Apples

Use firm apples such as Granny Smith or Golden Delicious for this recipe. Red Delicious and McIntosh don't hold up well against heat.

Some freshly ground black pepper is added to this recipe. It gives a little kick to the apples and complements the cinnamon.

1 cup unsalted butter	½ cup dark raisins
½ cup sugar	2 tablespoons Grand Marnier
¼ teaspoon ground allspice	(orange liqueur)
½ teaspoon ground cinnamon	¼ teaspoon freshly ground
2 cinnamon sticks	black pepper (optional)
4 cups firm apples, peeled,	
cored, and sliced	

Melt the butter and sugar in a medium-size saucepan over medium heat. Add the allspice, ground cinnamon, and cinnamon sticks and cook about 1 minute. Add the remaining ingredients, reduce the heat to low, cover, and simmer about 20 minutes or until the apples are soft.

Remove the cinnamon sticks and pour the cooked apples and their juices on a dessert plate.

Makes 4 servings.

Cherry and Strawberry Delight

I was about thirteen years old when I discovered my first cavity. I was eating some chocolate-covered cherry candy while watching television. The chocolate melted in my mouth and some of the liquid got into my cavity, causing major pain. A few weeks later, my dentist filled the cavity, and he also told me to lay off the chocolate-covered cherry candy. Although I never ate another piece of chocolate-covered cherry candy again, I do love cherry desserts.

½ cup sugar
2 cups half & half
4 cups fresh cherries, washed, stems removed, and pitted
2 cups fresh strawberries, washed and stems removed
1 teaspoon pure vanilla flavoring

⅓ cup vanilla liqueur
6 slices of toasted wheat bread, cut into quarters
½ gallon strawberry ice cream
¼ cup coarsely chopped unsalted roasted peanuts (for topping)

Place the sugar and half & half in a large saucepan over low heat, stirring constantly, until the sugar has dissolved. Add the remaining ingredients except the toasted wheat bread squares, ice cream, and chopped peanuts, reduce heat to low, cover, and cook about 15 minutes or until the fruit is soft, stirring frequently. Let cool to room temperature. Arrange the toasted wheat bread squares in a serving bowl. Scoop out the strawberry ice cream and place it on top, then add the cooked fruit mixture and sprinkle with nuts.

Makes 6 servings.

Cherry-Orange Stovetop Cobbler

If seasonal cherries are not available, frozen or canned cherries can be used. And pound cake crumbs can be substituted for the toasted cinnamon bread crumbs.

1 cup concentrated orange
    juice
6 cups fresh cherries, washed,
    stems removed, pitted,
    and coarsely chopped
1 teaspoon orange zest

2 cups coconut flakes
4 cups toasted cinnamon
    bread crumbs (preferably
    Pepperidge Farm brand)
¼ teaspoon ground cinnamon

Place the orange juice and about ¼ cup water in a large skillet and heat over medium heat about 2 minutes. Add the cherries and orange zest, cover, and simmer about 15 minutes, stirring occasionally. Stir in the coconut flakes and cook about 2 to 3 minutes longer. Most of the juice should have evaporated at this stage. If not, add more coconut flakes. Remove from heat, sprinkle bread crumbs and cinnamon on top, and place the skillet under a broiler until the topping slightly browns.

Makes 6 servings.

Easy Peach Cobbler

About 10 years ago, my novelist friend E. Lynn Harris came over to my home and ate what he called "a serious soul food dinner." We feasted on fried chicken, mixed mustard and turnip greens, macaroni and cheese, potato salad, cornbread, and sweet potatoes.

There were seven other good friends who also joined us that evening. We talked and laughed so much that I forgot to serve the peach cobbler dessert. I had placed it in the oven to keep warm, but totally forgot about it.

Well, here's a tasty top-of-the-stove peach cobbler recipe. You'll never need to put it in the oven — or forget about it.

¼ **cup unsalted butter**

2 **tablespoons all purpose flour**

½ **teaspoon ground cinnamon**

¼ **teaspoon ground nutmeg**

5 **cups freshly peeled and sliced peaches**

½ **cup sugar**

6 **2-inch yellow cakes or pound cake slices**

2 **tablespoons sugar for topping**

⅛ **teaspoon ground allspice for topping**

Melt the butter in a large, heavy-bottomed skillet or saucepan over medium heat. Using a wooden spoon, stir in the flour, cinnamon, and nutmeg. Gradually pour ¼ cup water and continue stirring until well mixed. Add the peaches and ½ cup sugar, reduce the heat to low, cover, and let simmer about 5 to 6 minutes. Place the cake slices on a baking sheet, then put the pan in the oven and broil about 1 minute or until the cake slices turn slightly brown. Place the browned slices on top of the peaches, sprinkle with sugar and allspice, cover, and let cook 5 minutes.

Makes 6 servings.

Hot Buttered Rum Cake

My friend, the late Mrs. Ruth Anderson (who lived to be ninety-eight), gave me some wonderful aged Jamaican rums she had collected over the years so I used some to make this dessert. If you don't have any bottles of aged rum in your cabinet, any Caribbean dark rum will work just fine.

2 cups (4 sticks) unsalted butter, room temperature

2 cups sugar

3 cups sifted all purpose flour

2 teaspoons baking powder

½ teaspoon salt

6 large eggs, room temperature

1 cup heavy cream

¼ cup dark rum

½ cup (1 stick) salted butter

3 cups Rum-Raisin Sauce, see recipe on page 137

Preheat the oven to 350 degrees F. Place the unsalted butter and sugar in a large mixing bowl and beat with an electric mixer until light and fluffy. In a separate medium-size bowl, sift together the flour, baking powder, and salt, and set aside. Beat the eggs, one at a time into the butter and sugar mixture. Gradually add the flour mixture to the butter and sugar mixture, alternating with the heavy cream. Fold in ¼ cup rum and mix well until the batter is smooth. Pour into a nonstick 10-inch tube pan or 9 x 4½-inch loaf pan. Bake about 90 minutes or until a toothpick inserted in the cake center comes out clean. Once cooked, remove the cake from the oven and let cool completely for about 25 minutes before removing from the pan.

In a 12-inch skillet, melt ½ cup salted butter over medium heat, add 2 cups of Rum-Raisin Sauce and cook, stirring, for about 3 minutes. Place the whole cake into the skillet and pour 1 cup of

Rum-Raisin Sauce on top. Reduce the heat to very low. Cover the cake with large pieces of foil and cook for about 3 to 4 minutes. Add a little more Rum-Raisin Sauce if the cake starts sticking to the skillet.

Makes 8 servings.

Orange Slice

Bread baking in an outdoor oven at a local restaurant in Luxor, Egypt—it is sometimes served as a dessert by adding sugar, nuts, and oranges.

When I visited Luxor, Egypt, about fifteen years ago, I had a wonderful dessert similar to this recipe. It was at a local restaurant that had been serving the same foods on its menu for over one hundred years. Their version of Orange Slice was made with dates and pears, and served cold. I add Grand Marnier to my version to help bring out the fruit flavors.

2 cups orange juice	2 tablespoons Grand Marnier
½ cup lemon juice	¼ teaspoon cornstarch
¼ cup lemon zest	½ cup chopped toasted
¼ cup sugar	walnuts
8 large oranges, peeled, and separated into slices	

Combine the orange juice, lemon juice, lemon zest, and sugar in a medium-size bowl, and stir together with a spatula until well mixed. Pour into a medium-size saucepan and heat over low heat until the sugar is melted. Add the orange slices and Grand Marnier, cover, and cook about 10 minutes. Stir in the cornstarch to thicken, and the toasted chopped walnuts. Remove the saucepan from heat, pour the cooked orange slices into a medium-size serving bowl, and let cool for about 15 minutes, then put in the refrigerator and chill for about 2 hours. Serve in dessert glasses or champagne glasses topped with Cool Whip topping and a cherry.

Makes 4 to 6 servings.

Peaches and Cream

About thirty-five years ago, my mother formed a friendship with a wonderful lady named Thelma Thomas, who lived in a very small town called Bourbon about 50 miles south of Clarksdale, Mississippi. My younger sister and I would spend our summers with her. I can still remember how great Thelma's food tasted. She grew all sorts of wonderful vegetables in her garden, and she was one of those great cooks who made everything from scratch.

Thelma had three large peach trees in her yard, which grew some of the largest and sweetest peaches I've ever bitten into. Making this recipe of Peaches and Cream takes me back to her delicious table.

1 cup all purpose flour	2 cups vegetable oil (for deep
2 cups confectioners	frying)
(powdered) sugar	½ cup (1 stick) unsalted
1 large egg	butter
1 cup whole milk	¼ cup peach liqueur or
6 large ripe peaches, peeled	vanilla liqueur
and cut unto quarters	½ cup sugar

Combine the flour and sugar together in a shallow pan or bowl; set aside. In a separate medium-size mixing bowl, beat the egg and milk together. Dredge the peach slices through the flour mixture, then roll them in the egg and milk mixture, then recoat them in the flour mixture. Heat the vegetable oil to 375 degreees F in a medium-size pot or saucepan and fry the coated peaches for about 1 minute or until they turn golden brown, then drain them on paper towels.

Put the butter, peach liqueur, and sugar in a large skillet and heat over medium heat until the butter and sugar melt. Add the deep fried peach slices, cover the skillet, and let simmer about 5 minutes, stirring occasionally. Serve in a dessert bowl or platter with scoops of whipping cream (recipe follows).

Makes 4 to 6 servings.

Whipping Cream Ingredients

2 cups heavy whipping cream   1 teaspoon pure vanilla
½ cup confectioners   flavoring
   (powdered) sugar

Place all the ingredients into a blender or food processor and blend about 1 or 2 minutes or until the cream thickens.

Makes about 2½ cups.

Prune Pudding

I think I was about nine years old when I ate an entire box of prunes. They were sweet tasting and I thought it would be a good substitute for candy (Mother didn't allow her children to eat much candy). After a few hours passed by, I spent the next few hours in the bathroom, much to my family's amusement.

Prunes are dried plums, which are considered natural laxatives. This recipe is kind, using only ½ cup of prunes to make 4 to 6 servings. However, if you dare to add more, be my guest.

6 cups stale French or Italian bread, cut into 1-inch cubes

1 cup sugar

½ teaspoon ground cinnamon

1 cup (½ stick) melted butter

1 cup coarsely chopped pecans

½ cup coarsely chopped prunes

4 cups whole milk

1 cup Chocolate Sauce, see recipe on page 135

Preheat the oven to 375 degrees F. Place the bread cubes, sugar, ground cinnamon, melted butter, chopped pecans, chopped prunes, and milk together in a bowl and stir until well combined. Pour the mixture into a well-buttered 7x7-inch baking pan or casserole dish. Bake about 40 minutes or until the pudding is firm. Remove the pan from the oven and let cool for 20 minutes. Cut the pudding into 4 large squares.

Pour 1 cup chocolate sauce in a large, heavy-bottomed skillet over medium heat and cook, stirring constantly, about 2 to 3 minutes until heated. Place the pudding squares in the hot chocolate sauce, reduce the heat to low, cover, and let cook about 3 minutes or until the pudding squares are heated through.

Makes 4 to 6 servings.

Rum-Raisin Pears

This recipe can be served warm or cold. I usually decide depending on the season I'm serving it in—summer, cold; winter, warm. Try using a firm pear that holds up to heat, such as Bosc, Seckel, or Kieffer.

½ cup (1 stick) unsalted
   butter
½ cup sugar
½ cup golden raisins
6 cups firm pears, peeled,
   cored, and sliced

2 tablespoons pear liqueur or
   vanilla liqueur
¼ teaspoon ground
   cardamom
1 cup Rum-Raisin Sauce, see
   recipe on page 137

Melt the butter and sugar in a medium-size saucepan over medium heat. Add the raisins, pears, pear liqueur, and cardamom. Cover the saucepan, reduce the heat to low, and simmer about 10 minutes, stirring occasionally.

Pour 1 cup Rum-Raisin Sauce over the pears and cook, uncovered, for 10 minutes. Serve immediately, or refrigerate and serve cool.

Makes 4 servings.

Spiced Cantaloupe

Firm apples or pears can be substituted for the cantaloupe used in this recipe. You can also cook and cool this recipe, then mix it in a blender with some crushed ice and serve as a refreshing chilled sweet beverage.

2 cups orange juice
1 teaspoon orange zest
¼ teaspoon ground cinnamon
⅛ teaspoon white pepper
⅛ teaspoon ground ginger
¼ cup sugar

1 large cantaloupe (about 6 cups), peeled, seeded, and coarsely chopped
1 cup Orange Sauce, see recipe on page 136

Heat the orange juice and orange zest in a large saucepan over high heat for about 3 minutes until hot. Stir in the ground cinnamon, white pepper, ground ginger, and sugar. Reduce heat to low, cover, and simmer about 2 minutes. Add the cantaloupe slices and Orange Sauce, cover, and cook 15 minutes. Serve warm or refrigerate about 2 or 3 hours and serve chilled.

Makes 4 to 6 servings.

Sweet Potatoes and Pecans

I've made this dish with white potatoes before, and it turned out very good. I've also used red-skinned potatoes.

½ cup (1 stick) unsalted
    butter
½ cup sugar
2 pounds large sweet
    potatoes, peeled and cut
    into 1-inch slices

½ teaspoon ground cinnamon
¼ teaspoon ground allspice
1 cup coarsely chopped
    pecans

Melt the butter and sugar in a large, heavy-bottomed skillet over medium heat. Add the sweet potatoes, ground cinnamon, and ground allspice and about 2 cups water, cover, and simmer about 30 minutes, stirring every 10 minutes. During the last 10 minutes of cooking time, remove the lid, and continue to cook until all the liquid has evaporated. Sprinkle the pecans over the top of the cooked sweet potatoes. Place skillet under the broiler and let the nuts brown slightly.

Makes 6 servings.

Sweet Potato Crunch

This recipe can be doubled for large gatherings. The Rum-Raisin Sauce on page 137 or the Orange Sauce on page 136 can be substituted for the Coffee Sauce used in this recipe.

1 pound large sweet potatoes,
  peeled and cut into 1½-
  inch cubes
¾ cup sugar
1½ cups apple juice
¼ teaspoon freshly grated
  mace or nutmeg

½ cup (1 stick) unsalted
  melted butter
1½ cups coarsely chopped
  walnuts (optional)
1½ cups coconut flakes
1 cup Coffee Sauce, see
  recipe on page 136

Place the sweet potato cubes, sugar, apple juice, and mace in a large skillet. Heat over low heat, cover, and let simmer 25 minutes or until the potatoes are semi-soft, stirring occasionally. Add the remaining ingredients, cover, and cook about 15 minutes longer. Place the skillet in a 450 degree F oven for 3 to 5 minutes or until the top becomes lightly browned and firm.

Makes 4 to 6 servings.

Sweet Potatoes and Apples

Toasted walnuts can be added to this recipe, along with some raisins.

2 medium-size sweet potatoes
(about 1½ pounds)
2 large cooking apples (such
as Granny Smith or
Bosc)

½ cup packed brown sugar
½ cup (1 stick) unsalted
butter
½ teaspoon ground cinnamon

Wash and peel the sweet potatoes, then cut them diagonally into ½-inch slices. Core and peel the apples and cut each into 8 wedges. Pour the sugar, ½ cup water, and butter into a large saucepan. Heat over medium heat until the sugar is completely melted. Add the sliced sweet potatoes and apples to the saucepan. Sprinkle in the ground cinnamon, reduce the heat to medium low, and cook about 30 minutes or until the potatoes and apples are tender, turning the sweet potatoes and apples every 10 minutes. Add more water if needed.

Makes 4 to 6 servings.

Strawberries and Rhubarb

Growing up in northwest Mississippi, I did not eat a lot of rhubarb. It's more popular in midwestern and New England dishes, mostly pies and preserves.

Rhubarb must be cooked, it's never eaten raw. The leaves are poisonous and usually removed before the stems are brought to the market.

1 pound rhubarb stems
1 cup sugar
2 tablespoons freshly
    squeezed lemon juice
1 cup raisins
3 cups fresh strawberries,
    washed, stems removed,
    and cut into halves,
    lengthwise

2 cups Strawberry Sauce, see
    recipe on page 138
6 slices of pound cake or
    yellow cake, cut into
    1-inch slices

Cut the rhubarb stems into 3-inch pieces. Cover them with about 3 cups of water in a medium-size saucepan, cover the pan, and cook over medium heat for about 25 minutes or until the rhubarb turns soft. Work the stems through a food mill or drum sieve and place the pureed rhubarb, sugar, lemon juice, raisins, and strawberry slices along with strawberry sauce in the saucepan. Cover and heat over low heat about 12 to 15 minutes. Place the pound-cake slices in a large saucepan, pour the rhubarb and strawberry sauce over the slices, cover, and heat about 2 to 3 minutes and serve.

Makes 6 servings.

5

Savory Sauces

Barbecue Sauce

ONCE THE BASIC ingredients (ketchup, sugar, black pepper, etc.) for making barbecue sauce have been picked out, it's very easy to create a variety of flavors. Some ideas include citrus-flavored barbecue sauce (adding fresh fruit) or roasted garlic–flavored barbecue sauce (adding roasted garlic cloves). This barbecue sauce recipe contains herbs, so it has an herbal (earthy) background taste. Recipe suggestions are on pages 17, 67, and 78.

2 cups ketchup
½ cup sugar
⅓ cup balsamic vinegar
1 tablespoon chopped fresh
    oregano
1 tablespoon chopped fresh
    rosemary

1 tablespoon chopped fresh
    sage
½ teaspoon mustard powder
½ teaspoon black pepper

Place all the ingredients in a small saucepan and add about ½ cup water. Bring to a boil over high heat, stirring constantly. Cover the saucepan, reduce the heat to low, and simmer about 10 minutes, stirring every 2 to 3 minutes.

Makes about 2¹/₂ cups.

Brown Sauce

This recipe is called Brown Sauce, but it's also a gravy. You can make a larger quantity and freeze it in an airtight container for future use. Recipe suggestions are on pages 35, 58, 77, and 83.

¹/₂ **cup all purpose flour**	1 **teaspoon salt**
¹/₄ **cup vegetable oil**	¹/₂ **teaspoon black pepper**

Pour the flour into a medium-size heavy-bottomed skillet and heat over medium heat until the flour turns light brown, about 10 minutes, stirring constantly. Add the oil and continue to stir about 3 minutes. Pour in about 4 cups water, add salt and black pepper, reduce the heat to low, and continue to stir about 5 minutes longer. For a thinner brown sauce, add more water.

Makes about 2¹/₂ cups.

Burgundy Sauce

Other wines such as Bordeaux, Cabernet Sauvignon, or Merlot can be substituted for the Burgundy wine used in this recipe. Just remember to rename the sauce after whatever wine you use.

Recipes using this wine sauce are on pages 76 and 99.

½ cup (1 stick) butter
2 tablespoons finely chopped shallots
1 tablespoon finely chopped garlic

1 cup finely chopped white button mushrooms
2½ cups Burgundy wine

Melt the butter in a medium-size saucepan over medium heat. Add the shallots and garlic and sauté about 2 minutes. Add the mushrooms and cook about 5 minutes, stirring constantly. Pour in the wine and stir well, reduce the heat to low, cover the saucepan, and let simmer about 15 minutes, stirring occasionally.

Makes about 2 cups.

Celery Sauce

This Celery Sauce recipe can also be used as a hearty vegetarian soup base or stock. A recipe suggestion is on page 49.

3 tablespoons butter
1½ cups finely chopped celery
1 cup finely chopped carrots
2 cups vegetable broth

½ teaspoon white pepper
3 dashes Tabasco sauce
1 teaspoon cornstarch (optional)

Melt the butter in a medium-size saucepan over medium heat. Add the celery and carrots and cook until they soften. Add the remaining ingredients except the cornstarch, cover the saucepan, reduce the heat to low, and cook about 15 minutes, stirring occasionally. Remove the saucepan from the heat and, if desired, stir in the cornstarch.

Makes about 3½ cups.

Creole Sauce

This Creole Sauce freezes well, when stored in an airtight container or re-sealable plastic freezer bag. Sometimes I puree this sauce in a blender or a food processor and use it as a liquid base for seafood gumbo, vegetarian gumbo, or beef stews.

Recipe suggestions are on pages 45 and 50.

½ cup (1 stick) butter
2 tablespoons vegetable oil
1 cup diced onions
1 cup diced celery
1 cup diced sweet green bell
   peppers
1 teaspoon dried thyme
4 cups diced tomatoes

1 tablespoon sugar
½ teaspoon black pepper
1 teaspoon Louisiana hot
   sauce
2 dashes Tabasco Sauce
   (optional)
1 cup vegetable broth

Heat the butter and oil in a large, heavy-bottomed skillet over medium heat for about 2 minutes until hot. Add the onions, celery, and sweet green bell peppers and cook for about 5 minutes or until they become soft, stirring constantly. Add the remaining ingredients, reduce the heat to low, and simmer for about 25 minutes, stirring frequently.

Makes about 6 cups.

Dill Sauce

A tarragon-flavored sauce can be made using the base ingredients in this recipe. Recipe suggestions are on pages 35 and 62.

2 tablespoons olive oil
¼ cup butter
⅓ cup finely chopped onions
  or shallots
3 tablespoons freshly
  squeezed lemon juice

½ cup capers, drained
½ cup chopped fresh dill
2 cups half & half
salt and black pepper to taste

Heat the oil and butter in a medium-size saucepan over medium heat until hot (but not smoky). Add the onions and sauté for about 1 minute. Reduce the heat to low, add the remaining ingredients, and cook about 15 minutes, stirring frequently.

Makes about 2½ cups.

Herbal Sauce

I use some of my favorite herbs in this sauce. Be creative and make your own version of Herbal Sauce, using your own favorite herbs. Recipe suggestions are on pages 35, 84, and 101.

2½ cups vegetable broth or
chicken broth
2 tablespoons butter
1 tablespoon chopped fresh
marjoram (or 1 teaspoon
dried)
1 tablespoon chopped fresh
rosemary (or 1 teaspoon
dried)

1 tablespoon chopped fresh
thyme (or 1 teaspoon
dried)
⅓ cup dry white wine
⅛ teaspoon white pepper
½ teaspoon cornstarch
(optional)

Place all the ingredients except the cornstarch in a small saucepan
and bring to a boil over high heat. Reduce the heat to low, cover the
saucepan, and simmer about 15 minutes, stirring occasionally. Remove the saucepan from the heat and, if desired, stir in the cornstarch.

Makes about 2¾ cups.

Mushroom Sauce

If possible, use only fresh mushrooms to make this sauce. Recipe
suggestions are on pages 28, 35, and 91.

3 tablespoons olive oil
½ cup finely chopped onions
1 cup finely chopped white
button mushrooms
1 cup finely chopped
portabella mushrooms

1 cup finely chopped oyster
mushrooms
2 cups vegetable or chicken
broth
salt and black pepper to taste

Heat the olive oil in a large saucepan over medium heat for about
1 minute or until hot (but not smoky). Add the onions and sauté
onions until they are soft. Add the mushrooms, broth, salt, and
pepper. Cover the saucepan with a lid and cook about 15 minutes.

Makes about 4½ cups.

Tomato Sauce

If fresh seasonal tomatoes are not available, use canned ones. Canned tomatoes are picked during peak season when their flavor is optimal. Suggestions for using this recipe are on pages 24 and 36.

¼ cup olive oil	¼ cup freshly chopped basil
1 cup diced onions	3 cups diced tomatoes
2 tablespoons freshly chopped garlic	½ teaspoon sugar
1 tablespoon fresh rosemary (or 1 teaspoon dried)	2 tablespoons freshly grated Parmesan cheese
	salt and black pepper to taste

Heat the oil in a large saucepan over medium heat for about 1 minute or until hot. Add the onions and sauté until they turn soft. Add garlic, rosemary, and basil and sauté for 3 minutes. Add the remaining ingredients to the saucepan, reduce the heat to low, cover the saucepan with a lid, and simmer for 30 minutes, stirring every 10 minutes. Pour the sauce into a bowl and let it cool to room temperature for about 1 hour. Pour the sauce into a blender or food processor and puree until the texture is smooth. Pour the pureed sauce back into the saucepan and heat until it's hot.

Makes about 3½ cups.

White Wine Sauce

I like to make this sauce, pour it into several ice trays, and freeze it for future use. It's a convenient way to add quick flavor to soups or marinades for poultry, fish, and vegetarian dishes. Recipe suggestions are on pages 34 and 61.

2 tablespoons butter	1 cup vegetable broth
½ cup finely chopped onions	3 cups dry white wine
½ cup finely chopped celery	salt and black pepper to taste

Melt the butter in a medium-size saucepan over medium heat. Sauté the onions and celery until they become soft. Add the vegetable broth, wine, salt, and pepper; reduce the heat to low, cover the saucepan with a lid, and let simmer about 30 minutes.

Makes about 4 cups.

6

Dessert Sauces

Chocolate Sauce

Raspberry (1 tablespoon) or mint (1 teaspoon) liqueurs can be added to this chocolate sauce recipe. Chopped unsalted, toasted pecans or unsalted roasted peanuts (about ¼ cup) can also be added.

A recipe suggestion for this chocolate sauce is on page 118.

12 ounces (about 12 squares) bittersweet chocolate, broken into pieces	2 cups sugar ¼ cup unsalted butter ¼ teaspoon salt

Place the chocolate and 1½ cups water in a small, heavy-bottomed saucepan and bring to boil over medium heat. Cook about 5 minutes, constantly stirring. Add the sugar and butter, and continue to stir about 5 minutes longer over medium heat. Stir in the salt and remove the saucepan from the heat.

Makes about 2¼ cups.

Coffee Sauce

For a stronger coffee flavor, substitute the same quantity of espresso for the coffee. A recipe suggestion for this Coffee Sauce is on page 123.

½ cup sugar
1 tablespoon cocoa powder
1 cup strong black coffee
½ cup evaporated milk

½ teaspoon pure vanilla
   flavoring
⅛ teaspoon salt

In a small bowl, mix together the sugar and cocoa powder and pour into a small saucepan. Add the coffee, evaporated milk, and about ¼ cup water. Heat slowly over low heat for about 10 minutes, constantly stirring. Add the vanilla flavoring and salt, and cook about 3 minutes.

Makes about 1½ cups.

Orange Sauce

Other fruit juice flavors such as lemon, lime, or tangerine can be used instead of orange. Combinations of fruits can also be used — such as strawberry and orange or something exotic like passion fruit and lime.

A recipe using this sauce is on page 121.

½ cup sugar
1½ teaspoons cornstarch
2 cups orange juice
2 teaspoons orange zest

1 tablespoon butter
1 tablespoon orange liqueur
   or Grand Marnier

Combine the sugar, cornstarch, and 1¼ cups water in a small, heavy-bottomed saucepan. Heat over low heat for 2 minutes, stirring constantly. Then add the orange juice, orange zest, butter, and Grand Marnier, cover, and cook about 8 to 10 minutes, stirring frequently every 2 minutes.

Makes about 2 cups.

Rum-Raisin Sauce

This sauce has a strong alcohol flavor, but you can burn off the alcohol by flambéing it. Tilt the saucepan to the flame on the stove after the rum has been added, or light a long match (used for a fireplace), and carefully hold it above the saucepan. Recipe suggestions for this sauce are on pages 114 and 120.

½ cup sugar
½ cup (1 stick) unsalted
    butter
2 cups heavy cream

⅛ teaspoon salt
½ cup raisins
¼ cup dark rum

Place the sugar and butter in a heavy-bottomed saucepan. Heat over medium heat for about 5 minutes or until a thick syrup has formed. Gradually stir in the cream and salt. Cook about 2 minutes. Then add the raisins and rum and cook 5 minutes, constantly stirring.

Makes 2½ cups.

Strawberry Sauce

Pineapple, mango, or papaya can be substituted for the strawberries. A recipe suggestion for this strawberry sauce is on page 124.

3 cups fresh strawberries, cut into halves	2 tablespoons fresh lemon juice
½ cup sugar	2 tablespoons whiskey

Place all the ingredients in a medium-size sauce pan. Bring to a boil over medium heat, occasionally stirring. Cover the sauce pan with a lid, reduce heat to low and let simmer about 15 minutes. Let fruit mixture cool completely, then place in a blender and puree about 1 minute.

Makes about 3 cups.

7

The Pantry

I THINK THE PANTRY is one of the most interesting rooms in the house. This small space can tell you so much about the people who live there. Are they amateur cooks or serious cooks? Do they eat out a lot or prepare and eat most meals at home? Are they one of those families who buy all of the latest trendy countertop kitchen gadgets or appliances, and hardly ever use them? Do they cook most of their meals from scratch?

I remember the first time I went to Santa Barbara, California, to visit my friend Julia Child. Her kitchen was very small, about 10'x12', with no pantry. But she had all kinds of kitchen gadgets, utensils, and pots and pans mounted on the walls. She told me that these things meant a great deal to her and that she'd had them for many, many years, in some cases since she launched her culinary career over fifty years earlier. Before moving out to California, Julia had downsized quite a bit. She sold her home in Cambridge, Massachusetts, and donated the bulk of her appliances, gadgets, utensils, pots, and pans to the Smithsonian — including the actual kitchen.

My kitchen is also small, and I, too, have most of my favorite gadgets, utensils, and pots and pans mounted on the walls. My culinary friends and family say it's a miracle that I can prepare a six-course meal for ten or twelve guests in such a small space. My kitchen is about 8'x 7'—the average size of a pantry in an average-size American home.

This chapter contains conversion and measurement charts that can be used as a reference guide when cooking. I've also provided lists of recommended kitchen appliances, cookware, bakeware, utensils, accessories, and cutlery, as well as a shopping guide for stocking up your pantry, kitchen cabinets, countertops, and the walls of your kitchen.

U.S. CONVERSION CHART

⅛ teaspoon	=	dash
½ teaspoon	=	30 drops
1 teaspoon	=	⅓ tablespoon or 60 drops
3 teaspoons	=	1 tablespoon or ⅓ fluid ounce
½ tablespoon	=	1½ teaspoons
1 tablespoon	=	3 teaspoons or ½ fluid ounces
2 tablespoons	=	1 fluid ounce
3 tablespoons	=	1½ fluid ounces
4 tablespoons	=	¼ cup or 2 fluid ounces
8 tablespoons	=	½ cup or 4 fluid ounces
12 tablespoons	=	¾ cup or 6 fluid ounces
16 tablespoons	=	1 cup or 8 fluid ounces or ½ pint
¼ cup	=	4 tablespoons or 2 fluid ounces
⅓ cup	=	5 tablespoons + 1 teaspoon
½ cup	=	8 tablespoons or 4 fluid ounces
¾ cup	=	12 tablespoons or 6 fluid ounces
1 cup	=	16 tablespoons or ½ pint or 8 fluid ounces
2 cups	=	1 pint or 16 fluid ounces
1 pint	=	2 cups or 16 fluid ounces
1 quart	=	2 pints or 4 cups or 32 ounces
1 gallon	=	4 quarts or 8 pints or 16 cups or 128 fluid ounces

METRIC CONVERSION CHARTS

Volume

¼ teaspoon	=	1.23 milliliters
½ teaspoon	=	2.46 milliliters
¾ teaspoon	=	3.70 milliliters
1 teaspoon	=	4.93 milliliters
1¼ teaspoons	=	6.16 milliliters
1½ teaspoons	=	7.39 milliliters
1¾ teaspoons	=	8.63 milliliters
2 teaspoons	=	9.86 milliliters
1 tablespoon	=	14.79 milliliters
1 fluid ounce	=	29.57 milliliters
2 tablespoons	=	29.57 milliliters
3 tablespoons	=	44.36 milliliters
¼ cup	=	59.25 milliliters
½ cup	=	118.3 milliliters
1 cup	=	236.59 milliliters
2 cups or 1 pint	=	473.18 milliliters
3 cups	=	709.77 milliliters
4 cups or 1 quart	=	946.36 milliliters
4 quarts or 1 gallon	=	3.785 liters

METRIC CONVERSION CHART

Weight

1 ounce	=	28.35 grams
4 ounces or ¼ pound	=	113.40 grams
6 ounces	=	170.1 grams
8 ounces or ½ pound	=	226.8 grams
12 ounces or ¾ pound	=	340.2 grams
16 ounces or 1 pound	=	453.6 grams
24 ounces or 1½ pounds	=	680.4 grams
32 ounces or 2 pounds	=	907.0 grams
2 pounds + 3 ounces	=	1 kilogram or 1000 grams

Abbreviations

US/UK

oz	=	ounce
lb	=	pound
in	=	inch
ft	=	foot
tsp	=	teaspoon
tb	=	tablespoon
fl oz	=	fluid ounce
qt	=	quart

Metric

g	=	gram
kg	=	kilogram
mm	=	millimeter
cm	=	centimeter
ml	=	milliliter
l	=	liter

TEMPERATURE CONVERSION CHART

To convert Fahrenheit to Celsius, subtract 32, multiply by 5, and divide by 9. To convert from Celsius to Fahrenheit, multiply by 9, divide by 5, and add 32.

Fahrenheit	Celsius
100	40
125	50
150	70
175	80
200	95
225	110
250	120
275	135
300	150
325	165
350	180
375	190
400	205
425	220
450	230
475	245
500	260

KITCHEN COUNTERTOP APPLIANCES

The Basics

Blender

Can opener

Coffee grinder

Coffee pot

Electric knife

Food processor

Frozen dessert maker

Hand mixer

Juicer

Microwave

Pressure cooker

Slow cooker

Stand mixer

Toaster

Waffle maker

Beyond the Basics

Bread maker

Coffee mill

Convection steamer

Crème brulee set

Electric kettle

Electric weight scale

Electric skillet

Espresso machine

Immersion blender

Mini prep-food processor

Plate warmer

Rice cooker

Rotisserie

Salad spinner

Toaster oven broiler

Cookware

This cookware can be purchased in anodized aluminum, cast iron, enamel, hard anodized nonstick, porcelain, or stainless steel. Buy size and quantity to your discretion.

The Basics

Butter warmer

Colander

Covered casserole dish

Covered sauté pan

Dutch oven

Frying pan

Mixing bowls

Omelete pan

Roasting pan

Saucepan

Saute pan

Steamer with lid

Stock pot

Tea kettle

Wire rack

Beyond the Basics

Chef's pan

Covered braiser

Covered saucepan

Crepe pan

Double boiler

Flan pan

Fondue set

Grill pan

Hotel pan

Lasagne pan

Oval skillet

Panini pan

Petite casserole

Souffle pan

Wok

Bakeware

This bakeware can be purchased in aluminized steel, hard anodized, hard anodized nonstick, or heavy-gauge aluminum. Buy size and quantity to your discretion.

The Basics

Cookie sheet

Cooling racks

Large roaster

Muffin pan

Nonstick oven liners

Pizza pan

Pie pan

Sheet cake pan

Square cake pan

Round cake pan

Beyond the Basics

6 in 1 loaf pan

Angel food pan

Fluted cake pan

Jelly roll pan

Madeleine pan

Mini madeleine pan

Mini tart pan

Nonstick baking mat

Springform pan

Tart pan

Utensils and Accessories

Most of these utensils and accessories can be purchased in nylon, silicone, or stainless steel.

The Basics

Cheese grater

Cotton apron

Cotton or silicone oven mitts

Cotton towels

Fork

Garlic press

Ice cream scoop

Ladle

Measuring cup set

Measuring spoon set

Meat mallet

Melon baller

Pasta fork

Potato peeler

Potato masher

Rolling pin

Spatula

Slotted turner

Tongs

Whisk

Beyond the Basics

Basting spoon

Blender cloth cover

Bowl scraper

Butter cutter

Channel tool

Cheese slicer

Dish cloth scrubber

Flat grater

Food mill

Lemon zester

Lobster and crab picks

Mixing spatula

Pastry brush

Pizza slicer

Potato ricer

Short turner

Silicone jar opener

Skimmer

Thermometer

Tomato knife

Cutlery

Knives are made of a combination of steel and carbon. A higher ratio of carbon makes a sharper knife.

The Basics	Beyond the Basics
Boning knife	Asian knife
Bread knife	Carving set (knife-fork)
Carving knife	Fluting knife
Chef's knife	Magnetic strip
Cleaver	Mincing knife
Cutting board	Pâté knife
Paring knife	Poultry shears
Scissors	Salmon slicer
Sharpening steel	Serrated pairing knife
Wooden block knife holder	Steak knife set

Shopping Guide

Company	Website	Telephone
Allclad:	*www.allclad.com*	1-800-255-2523
Apilco:	*www.apilco.com* (Paris, France)	1-33-0-1 42 46 43 74
Berndes:	*www.berndes.com*	1-888-266-6983
Braun:	*www.braun.com*	1-800-272-8611
Calphalon:	*www.calphalon.com*	1-800-809-7267
Cuisinart:	*www.cuisinart.com*	1-800-726-0190
Dupont:	*www.dupont.com*	1-866-205-1664
Jahenckels:	*www.jahenckels.com*	1-800-777-4308
KitchenAid:	*www.kitchenaid.com*	1-800-541-6390
LeCreuset:	*www.lecreuset.com*	1-877-273-8738
OXO:	*www.oxo.com*	1-800-545-4411
SunBeam:	*www.sunbeam.com*	1-800-458-8407
T-Fal:	*www.t-falusa.com*	1-800-395-8325
Viking Range:	*www.vikingrange.com*	1-888-845-4641
Wuesthof:	*www.wuesthof.de*	1-800-289-9878
Chefs Catalog:	*www.chefscatalog.com*	1-800-884-2433
Crate and Barrel:	*www.crateandbarrel.com*	1-800-967-6696
Sur la Table:	*www.surlatable.com*	1-800-243-0852
Williams Sonoma:	*www.williamssonoma.com*	1-877-812-6235

8

Entertaining and Traveling

My MOTHER was the official hostess in my family. Most of the big dinners were held at our house, and usually took place during the major holidays.

Mother took charge of all the hard-to-make dishes. She would assign her children smaller, less complicated tasks such as peeling boiled potatoes to make potato salad or turning the ice cream maker by hand to make homemade vanilla ice cream.

Our Thanksgiving and Christmas dinners would sometimes take up to two days of preparation time. The first step would be putting together the menu. We would have discussions around what traditional foods we'd include, such as roast turkey, ham, dressing, mixed turnip and mustard greens, fried corn, string beans, rolls, sweet potato pie, and coconut cake. After the menu items were selected, the next step was grocery shopping. This stage was always fun. I always volunteered to do the marketing with Mother. We would make stops at various specialty meat markets and regular grocery stores. When we returned home from our shopping, Mother would spend time deciding who would be invited to dinner—she usually would invite other members of our family and some extended family members (what we called long-time friends of the family).

Next, Mother would start pulling out china, serving platters, tablecloths, and napkins, and start working on her color scheme. If the dinner was to be a buffet, all the main dishes would be placed on the dining room table and we would serve ourselves and sit in the dining room or living room. If the dinner was to be more formal, one of my sisters would set the table and we would serve the food family-style.

From time to time, Mother would add at least one new dish to our traditional menu. We would call it her experimental dish, which sometimes came out fairly well, but other times, it was a disaster like when she made a large pot of seafood gumbo, using only a handful of small cocktail shrimp. It was the only seafood in the gumbo. All the family members laughed about it.

After consulting with some of my close culinary friends, I decided to include an entertainment chapter in this book as a practical guide for easy entertaining, from informal coffee get-togethers to a formal dinner party for twelve guests.

There's also a section on wine pairing that provides basic information about how to pair wines with some of your favorite foods. And finally, there's a travel destination section that lists all of the eateries, cooking schools, small towns, cities, and countries mentioned in this book.

Come Over for Coffee

From time to time, I like to invite a friend or two over to my home for coffee. This gives us time to talk about world events, family, politics, and gossip in the food industry. I call this get together "Come over for coffee."

Over the past ten years, Americans have developed a palate for gourmet coffee. I remember back in the early 1970s when the American coffee industry was dominated by three or four national brands. The coffee was average tasting and very expensive.

My grandmother never lived to see how the national coffee chains changed the way Americans drink coffee. She died in 1978. However, it brings a smile to my face when I think about how much she would have enjoyed a nice espresso on an early Sunday morning in Clarksdale, Mississippi, while reading the weekend paper. Now, I'm also a lover of strong coffee. But I like mine black with sugar or sugar substitute. Grandmother always sweetened her black coffee with one or two teaspoons of sugar.

Today, there are so many wonderful brands and flavors of coffees on the market, priced much more reasonably.

Some of my favorite coffee beans come from Ethiopia (Arabica coffee), grown in the wild trees in the provinces of Djimmah, Sidamio, Lekepti and Salo; Hawaii (kona coffee), grown on volcanic soil; Kenya (also Arabica coffee), grown at high elevations (15,000 feet plus); and Brazil (Robusta coffee), from the hills of Mogiana in São Paulo. The Brazilian Robusta coffee bean makes great foam on espresso drinks.

I usually buy my coffee beans roasted and whole, and store them in an airtight container in the refrigerator or freezer.

Café au Lait

1¼ cups strong coffee 1¼ cups whole milk (or skim milk)

Heat the coffee and milk in 2 separate small pots until they begin to boil. Then simultaneously pour the coffee and milk into mugs.

Makes 2 servings.

Iced Coffee

2 cups warm (not hot) coffee	2 scoops vanilla ice cream or
2 tablespoons heavy cream or	chocolate ice cream
milk	

Pour the warm coffee into 2 12-oz. iced tea glasses. Add 1 table-spoon heavy cream and about 4 ice cubes to each glass and stir well. Then add a scoop of vanilla ice cream on top of the cubes in each glass.

Makes 2 servings.

Come over for Coffee, Menu One

Sweet Potato Crunch, see recipe on page 123
2 cups Café Au Lait

Come Over for Coffee, Menu Two

Mixed Berry Cobbler, see recipe on page 106
2 glasses Iced Coffee

Breakfast

There's nothing better than having a nice southern-style home-made breakfast—in bed. I always look forward to visiting my good friends in southern Indiana because they serve me break-fast in bed—what a treat. My favorite dishes would be seasonal fresh fruit, blueberry muffins served with lots of butter, scram-bled eggs with cheddar cheese, a few slices of fried pork bacon, and a fresh pot of strong coffee. This breakfast feast reminds me of spending the weekends with my grandmother, Ruth Randle, and great-grandmother, Ada Penn, who made wonderful breakfast feasts.

Breakfast Menu One

Buttered Brown Potatoes, see recipe on page 19
Smothered Chicken, see recipe on page 81
Fresh seasonal fruit
Biscuits or rolls with butter, honey, or jam
Fresh coffee or juice

Breakfast Menu Two

Potato Croquettes and Gravy, see recipe on page 35
Chicken Fried Steak, see recipe on page 82
Buttery Cinnamon Apples, see recipe on page 110
Rolls or cornbread
Fresh coffee or juice

Brunch

I started hosting brunches at my home about twenty years ago. Before then, I hosted mostly cocktail parties and dinner parties.

My mother rarely made brunches, but when she did, it would be for a special occasion, like when out-of-town relatives were visiting. Mother's menu would include delicious fried chicken, twice-baked potatoes, fresh fried corn, mixed green salad, and a pound cake or chocolate cake. Whenever she ran short on time, she would use a store-bought cake mix and doctor it up by adding additional ingredients to make it taste as if it were made from scratch. From time to time she would use the store-bought frosting, sometimes even on homemade cakes. The entire family thought it was delicious, especially the Dutch chocolate, milk chocolate, and lemon flavors.

Champagne Brunch, Menu One

Mimosa

Orange Blossom

Green Beans with Onions and Bacon, see recipe on page 30

Rolls or Biscuits

Salmon Steaks, see recipe on page 55

Blackberries and Dumplings, see recipe on page 108

Coffee and tea

Mimosa

12 ounces chilled dry
    champagne
12 ounces chilled orange juice

4 whole strawberries
4 orange slices

Pour 3 ounces of dry chilled champagne into each of 4 chilled champagne flutes. Then pour 3 ounces of orange juice into each glass. Drop a strawberry into each glass and decorate the rim with a slice of orange.

Makes 4 servings.

Orange Blossom

4 ounces gin
2 ounces triple sec (orange-
    flavored liqueur)

8 ounces chilled orange juice

Fill a large martini shaker with ice. Add the gin, triple sec, and orange juice. Shake and strain into 4 chilled cocktail glasses.

Makes 4 servings.

Southern-Style Brunch, Menu Two

Mint Julep
Sparkling Wine Julep
Green Pea and Carrot Croquettes, see recipe on page 34
Skillet Cornbread
Buttered Kale, see recipe on page 20
Banana Whip, see recipe on page 105
Coffee, tea

Mint Julep

24 fresh mint leaves   8 ounces bourbon
2 ounces sugar syrup (a 50/50
    mixture of water and
    granulated sugar)

Place 6 fresh mint leaves in each of 4 chilled cocktail glasses. Add the sugar syrup and mash the leaves with a large tablespoon for 30 seconds. Pour 2 ounces of bourbon in each glass, then fill with crushed ice, stir, and serve.

Makes 4 servings.

Sparkling Wine Julep

8 sprigs of fresh mint
4 tablespoons sugar syrup (a
50/50 mixture of water
and granulated sugar)

8 ounces brandy
8 ounces chilled dry sparkling
wine or champagne

Place 2 sprigs of mint in each of 4 chilled champagne glasses. Add 1 tablespoon of sugar syrup to each glass and stir well. Then pour 2 ounces brandy and 2 ounces chilled sparkling wine into each glass. Fill with ice, stir well, and serve.

Makes 4 servings.

Wine Pairing

Selecting the perfect wine for a brunch, lunch, or dinner can be complicated, especially when the host doesn't know much about wines. The easiest route to take is to ask the wine merchant what wines would best pair with the menu to be served. If you take this route, I suggest letting the wine merchant take a look at the recipe so that the ingredients used and cooking techniques complement the wine selection even better. Here's some basic information that can be used as a reference when shopping for wines.

White Wine—wine without any red color or pink color. White wines fall into three main taste categories (not including sparkling or sweet wines).

1. Dry (not sweet) and crisp. Examples: White Italian wines or some French white wines.
2. White wines that are dry and full bodied yet oaky (because

of their contact with oak barrels). Full bodied are weigh of the wine on the tongue There are three ranges: light-bodied, medium-bodied, or full-bodied. Examples of dry and full-bodied wine with oaky taste: California chardonnay and French Burgundy wines.

3. White wines that are medium-dry (but not bone dry), such as Riesling or Zinfandel.

Six common white wines are: Chablis, Chardonnay, Pinot Gris, Riesling, and Sauvignon Blanc.

Red wines—made from red or blush grapes (also called black grapes). The red color occurs when the colorless juice of the grapes sits in contact with the red grape skin during fermentation, which also gives the wine tannins, an important influence on the taste of red wine.

Red wine has three main taste categories.

1. Light-bodied fruity red wines with not much tannin, such as some French Beaujolais wines (picked during the first harvest).

2. Medium-bodied, moderately tannic red wines, such as less-expensive wines from the Bordeaux region in France or some of the less-expensive Italian Merlots.

3. Full-bodied tannic red wines, such as the best Bordeaux wines and the most expensive Californian Cabernet Sauvignons.

Six common red wines are: Beaujolais, Bordeaux, Burgundy, Cabernet Sauvignon, Merlot, and Pinot Noir.

Wine is a very complex beverage. It should be looked at and smelled before it is tasted. Follow this simple technique after pouring the wine.

1. Tilt your glass away from you and look at the color of the wine against a white background such as a piece of paper or tablecloth. Take note of the color of the wine (how pale or dark it is).
2. Set your glass on the table and swirl it so that the air becomes mixed with the wine, then bring the glass to your nose quickly and sniff the wine to smell the aroma.
3. Take a small sip of wine and hold it in your mouth. Open your lips and draw in some air across your tongue on top of the wine. Then swish the wine around your mouth as if you were chewing it, then swallow it. This whole process should take just a few seconds.

Note that different parts of the tongue have specialized tasting sensations. Sweetness is perceived on the front of the tongue, sourness on the sides, and bitterness across the rear of the tongue. When the wine is moved around the tongue, it has a chance to hit all the taste buds on the tongue.

Fruity or Sweet

When a wine is described as fruity, it has distinct aromas of fruit, as detected by the nose. When a wine is described as sweet, it is perceived as such by the tongue. If you have problems distinguishing fruity from sweet, hold your nose when you taste the wine. If the wine is sweet, you will be able to taste the sweetness, but not to smell the fruitiness.

Acidity or Tannin

All wines contain acid (tartaric acid that comes from the grapes). Acidity is the backbone of white wines. It gives the wine firmness and definition in your mouth. Tannins refer specifically to red wines. If you sip a dark red wine and it gives your mouth a drying-out feeling, that's tannin. It also reminds me of sipping a strong cup of hot tea, where that same drying sensation occurs. The tannins in red wines are described as soft, firm, or bitter.

Body

The body of wine refers to the impression of weight and size of the wine in your mouth. The wine can be described as fuller, bigger, or heavier. Other terms are light-bodied, medium-bodied, or full-bodied.

Food and Wine Pairing Basic Guideline

1. High-acid foods pair well with high-acid wines
2. Fatty foods containing lots of proteins pair well with tannic wines
3. Salty foods pair well with high-alcohol-content wines
4. Deep fried foods pair well with crisp, high-acid wines
5. Spicy foods pair well with low alcohol, low tannic wines

Examples of Food and Wine Pairing

1. Herb dressing—Sauvignon Blanc, Red Zinfandel
2. Cream butter sauces—Chardonnay, White Burgundies
3. Oysters, mussels—Pinot Grigio
4. Grilled, smoky meats—Shiraz
5. Salmon, lobster—Oaky Chardonnay
6. Trout, sole, shrimp—Non-oaky Chardonnay, Riesling
7. Beef, game—Cabernet, Merlot
8. Pizza, pasta, and red sauce—Zinfandel, Syrah, Chardonnay
9. Fried foods—Riesling, White Zinfandel, sparkling wines
10. Ethnic foods—Riesling, Chenin Blanc, White Zinfandel, sparkling wines

Dinner Parties

I enjoy hosting dinner parties because it gives me an opportunity to be creative with the menu and with selecting the kinds of drinks, wine pairings, and table settings. It usually takes me about two days of preparation to put together a nice dinner party. I'm one of those hosts who likes to do as much work in advance as I can so that I can really relax at the dinner party, mixing and mingling with my guests and sitting down to enjoy the meal with them. In order for me to do this, it is very important that I have everything organized and put together hours before my guests arrive. Here's an easy guideline to follow so that you too can enjoy your own dinner party with your guests.

Breaking bread with Charlotte Lyons, Donna Hodge,
and Jamie Oliver.

ANTOINETTE FIELDS

Family celebrating together—cousin Christine Randle's
50th birthday and Wilbert Jones's 40th.

Selecting Your Guests

I like to put together a guest list of friends and colleagues with
different professional career backgrounds and ethnicities. Sometimes, however, I put together a guest list of people who have a lot
in common. I've had dinner parties with only cookbook authors,
or food manufacturers, or even medical doctors.

Choosing the Date

Telephone each guest or mail out invitations about twenty days in advance. Request that the guests reply within one week of the dinner party.

Putting Together Your Menu

Putting together a theme menu can be easy. Some of my popular dinner party themes have been Country French, South African, New Orleans Creole, and Soul Food. Once I've selected my theme country, region, or city, I usually put together a menu of signature dishes, then I choose the right cocktail drinks and wine pairings. I also put together a table setting that reflects the theme, including tablecloth, napkins, plates, serving dishes, and flowers for the dining room table that fit the color scheme or pattern.

Checklist for the day before the dinner party

> Write out menu
> Select the linens (tablecloth, napkins, placemats, and place cards)
> Select the plates, silverware, and glassware
> Select the centerpieces and flowers
> Select the serving platters and serving utensils
> Set the dining room table

Checklist for the day of the dinner party

> Check the bathroom that the guests will be using. (Make sure there's enough tissue, hand towels, soap, and hand cream)
> Check the closet that the guests will be using (to make sure hangers and enough space are available)
> Check the stereo equipment and select music such as jazz, contemporary jazz, blues, or classical music

Dinner Party Game

About ten years ago, I created this fun game that I named WJ's Getting to Know You Game. Twelve questions are written on slips of paper, which are then carefully folded and placed in a small box. Each dinner guest gets to shake the box first, then pick one question, read it out loud, and answer the question. After the question has been answered by the guest, the remainder of the guests can comment on the answer. This game generates some conversations from your dinner guests.

If you are having a dinner party where most of the guests don't know each other, I suggest playing the game at the dinner table while eating. However, if your guests do know each other, I suggest playing the game after dinner, but pass the questions out before eating. This gives the guests plenty of time to think about their questions and put some serious thought into their answers.

Here are some sample questions. WJ's Getting to Know You Game.

1. What is your favorite place in the world to visit? Why?
2. If you could solve one problem in the world, what would it be? Why?
3. What book have you read lately?
4. What famous person looks like you?
5. What is the most risky thing that you have done and gotten away with?
6. What two subjects do you avoid discussing with others?
7. What food do you totally dislike? Why?
8. Who is your favorite actor? Why?
9. If you had one wish, what would it be? Why?
10. Have you ever told a secret that you promised to keep? What happened?

Creole-Style Dinner Party, Menu One

Social Mix and Mingle Appetizers and Cocktail

Fresh oysters on the half shell, served with horseradish, cocktail sauce, and fresh lemon slices

Toasted pecan halves, seasoned with garlic salt

Creole Bloody Mary

Sit-down Dinner Menu

Mixed green salad with Herbal Sauce, see recipe on page 131

Creamed Onions, see recipe on page 28

Crawfish Étoufée, see recipe on page 46

Chicken Creole, see recipe on page 79

French bread

Bananas with Pecans & Whiskey, see recipe on page 104

Wine Pairing Suggestions

Sauvignon Blanc (mixed green salad and Creamed Onions)

Riesling (Crawfish Etoufee)

Chenin Blanc (Chicken Creole)

Coffee (Creole coffee recommended, which is coffee brewed from ground coffee beans and chicory roots, also known as New Orleans coffee)

Creole Bloody Mary

¼ cup ice cubes
2 ounces vodka
4 ounces tomato juice
½ ounce lemon juice
2 drops Worcestershire sauce
⅛ teaspoon (a pinch) celery
    salt

2 to 3 dashes Tabasco sauce
1 celery stalk or 1 spiced
    green bean, for
    garnishing

Place all the ingredients in a chilled cocktail glass and stir well with a large tablespoon. Note: This recipe can be scaled up to make several drinks at once.

Makes 1 serving.

Low Country Dinner Party, Menu Two

Social Mix and Mingle Appetizer and Cocktail

Succotash (served chilled in martini glasses), see recipe on
    page 39
Chilled champagne

Sit-down Dinner Menu

Low Country Shrimp and Rice, see recipe on page 50
Smothered Rabbit, see recipe on page 97
Potato Croquettes and Gravy, see recipe on page 35
Biscuits
Peaches and Cream, see recipes on page 117

Wine Pairing Suggestions

Chardonnay (Low Country Shrimp and Rice)
White Burgundy (Smothered Rabbit and Potato Croquettes)
Coffee
After-dinner drink: Baileys or Kahlua, served on the rocks

Traveling

Here's a contact list of restaurants, clubs, and museums that inspired me to write this book. If you have an opportunity to visit any or all of them, I hope you enjoy them as much as I love them.

Clarksdale, Mississippi

Delta Blues Museum, 662-627-6820
  (www.deltabluesmuseum.org)
Ground Zero Blues Club, 662-621-9009
  (www.groundzerobluesclub.com)
Madidi Fine Dining Restaurant, 662-627-7007
  (www.madidires.com)

New Orleans, Louisiana

Brennan's Restaurant, 504-525-9711
  (www.brennansneworleans.com)
Commander's Palace, 504-896-7600
  (www.commanderspalace.com)
K-Pauls, 504-524-7394 (www.kpauls.com)

Hot Springs, Virginia

The Homestead Resort, 540-839-2832
  (www.thehomestead.com)

Chicago, Illinois

Edna's Restaurant & Catering Services, 773-638-7079
Kendall College, 312-752-2000 (www.kendall-college.com)

New York, New York

Sylvia's Restaurant, 212-996-0660
(www.sylviassoulfood.com)

Fairbanks, Alaska

Santa's Smokehouse, 907-456-3885
(www.santassmokehouse.com)

Paris, France

Ecole de Gastronomique Francaise Ritz-Escoffier (Cooking
School), 33-01-43-16-30-50 (www.ritzparis.com)
La Closerie des Lilas Restaurant, 33-01-40-51-34-50

Index

About the Author

ANTOINETTE FIELDS

WILBERT JONES attended the Ecole de Gastronomique Française Ritz-Escoffier in Paris and was a food scientist at Kraft General Foods. He is the president of Healthy Concepts, Inc., a food and beverage product and development company founded in 1993. He lives in Chicago.